Children's Glass Dishes, China, and Furniture

Volume II

DORIS ANDERSON LECHLER

COLLECTOR BOOKS
A Division of Schroeder Publishing Co., Inc.

Additional books by Doris Anderson Lechler:
Toy Glass
English Toy China
French and German Dolls, Dishes and Accessories

Doris Anderson Lechler
949 E. Cooke Road
Columbus, Ohio 43224

Additional copies of this book may be ordered from:

Collector Books
P.O. Box 3009
Paducah, KY 42002-3009

@ $19.95 Add $2.00 for postage and handling.

Dedication

Dedicated to my mother, Elizabeth Hall Anderson,
for smoothing the edges of my life.

Acknowledgments

The work involved in gathering endless details and pictures for a book on children's china, glass, furniture and playhouse accessories must be a joint effort comprised of past researchers, authors, current dealers, collectors, relatives and friends. No one person can know it all, find it all, or own it all; therefore I would like to give special recognition to the following people: Andrew P. Lechler, Elizabeth Hall Anderson, Ruth E. Smith, Joyce and Seth Johnston, Nancy Lubberger, Kay Hamilton, Betty Salzgaber, Florajane Steffen, Blanche Largent, Jerry and Sandy Schmoker, Carolyn Nelson, Mr. Lynn Welker, Dauphene and Howard Lundquest, Max and Helen Lundquest, Nancy Bellville, Linda Klies, MINIATURE NEWS subscribers, Catherine Landskov, Tom Neale and Glen Schlotfeldt, Ileen Schumaker, Helen and Roy Simmons, Laura and Andy Hartzfeld, Gene Austin, Nina Baugh, Pegge, Terry and Linda Gardner, Jeanetta and Ervin Freshour, Zoe and Jim Nonemaker, Rosario Tripepi, the GLASS REVIEW, the ANTIQUE TRADER, the DOLL AND TOY (from England), the Corning Glass Museum Library and museum office staff, the Ohio State Department of Photography and Cinema -- especially Tom Maloy, Clara Murray, Ruth Maehling, Betty O' Brien and Katie Miller; Bruce and Sheri Knight, Jean Dorney, Ernie and Gloria Schultz, Janet and Gale Fredrick, Joan and Ed Eisele.

Front Cover Photo

Shelf, left to right: Early Flow Blue tea set; ornate cranberry and enamel tumble up; biscuit jar; Mary Gregory amber beverage set.

Top of bookcase secretary: Kate Greenaway (style) beverage set with six (punch cup size) cups: secretary made of various fruit wood, bookcase top, fall down desk, two drawers and a cupboard base.

Inside secretary: top shelf, left to right: Wagon Wheel Staffordshire teas set and mug; sapphire and enamel, handled tumble up.

Second Shelf: Staffordshire Blue Willow teapot; Blue Blossom London (shape) teapot; Persian teapot (see complete sets in regular text).

Cane Rocker with stenciled back; doll.

Table Top: Asiatic Birds dinner set, Flow Blue, by Charles Meigh; four-branch glass candelabrum; Baby Thumbprint cake stand; Girl in a Ring caster holder with four matching bottles in the Block pattern; blue (onion style) flatware; goblets from the Enameled Leaf and Vine decanter set; feather tree from the Gardner collection.

Window: Copeland Christmas Holly pitcher and bowl; Wedgewood pitcher and bowl; English Lemonade set; child-size dry sink.

Floor: Child's picnic basket with Mary Gregory (canary) tumble up and ruby glass tea set; art glass tumble up with handled tumbler; Black Birds, six piece chanber set; child's slate lap desk with all original equipment; child's dresser set with painting on porcelain pieces in original box; toy bushel basket; Dream Baby in wicker buggy.

Under the table: Pot metal (type) tea set on a tray, all original and complete.

Window (top): A miniature chandelier in glass, one of a pair.

Most items are shown and described in the main text: Chair, doll, Dream Baby, buggy, basket and feather tree from the Gardner collection.

All other items are from the Lechler collection.

Back Cover Photo

Top shelf left to right: Miniature epergne, bristol vase, Du Berry tumble up, (2) London (shaped) teapots, Petite Square vase, Palm Leaf and Fan cake plate.

Second Shelf, left to right: Custard epergne, Dresden tete-a-tete set, amethyst tumble up, Minton porcelain tea set with two pots.

Window: Asbestos (type) chicken on a nest; early.

Floor, left to right: Night stand, 13¼" tall, 10½" across, two drawers; Humphrey's Clock compote; German toy decanter set; cane rocker with original stenciled pictures; doll; fashion umbrella; sewing basket; toy bath tub with hand painted violet trim; fully jointed, early bear in the tub; wagon of bears from the Gardner collection; W.S. Transfer wagon; Teddy Roosevelt Bear carrying a big stick (he dances). Bears, night stand, chair, doll, chicken, umbrella and wagon, Gardner collection.

China, glass, decanter set, compote, sewing basket and bath tub, Lechler collection.

About the Author

In her first two books, Doris concentrated heavily on children's glass dishes, with the second book emphasizing German toy china and toy furniture. In this, her third book, she turns her attention to English toy china and playhouse toys and accessories. She has made the shift in attention with her ususal zeal, partly because there were so many previously unpublished sets of toy china, at least in one publication, and partly because of a personal challenge. Now, you see the results. In doing this book, Doris has not only uncovered some remarkable sets, she has also discovered a fondness for the old English toy china. In fact, her collection of toy china nearly equals the toy glass collection and it is a direct result of the challenge of this book.

In addition to the three books, Doris writes for the ANTIQUE TRADER, the INSIDER, and the DOLL AND TOY magazine published in England. She continues to write the MINIATURE NEWS, a newsletter for collectors of children's toy glass, china, furniture and accessories. 1985 began the fifth year for this informal newsletter which has encouraged three miniature conventions as well as an "antiquing" tour which I'll never forget because of the wonderful people we had with us. It is remarkable to see so many collectors from diverse backgrounds, circumstances and geographic locations unite and work so well in a common field of interest. They are a wonderful group of friends. Doris has found their help essential and of course, it is appreciated by both of us.

Doris had a wonderful trip to England this year, buying special items for this book. She generated so much excitement about London that I intend to go with her in the spring.

Doris, her mother, and I run a considerably quieter establishment now that one son is married, one has his own apartment, and one twenty-year-old cat ran away from home late one night. (We were fortunate enough to be left with one wild cat and a very large dog.)

1985 began Doris's twenty-seventh year of teaching. She is a busy person who is, most of all my first, last, and most loving wife. She intends for me to stay as busy as she is and if I sit for more than an hour in front of the television, she is sure that I will atrophy.

Andy Lechler

Page 12 - EARLY MUGS & PLATES

Mugs#1 -
"Holy Scriptures..." $150.00-185.00
"The Path Of Truth..." $150.00-185.00
"Faith..." $150.00-185.00
#2 - Cat & Bonnet $100.00-125.00
Cats At Play $100.00-125.00
Cat Accident $100.00-125.00
Boy & Dog $100.00-125.00

Page 13
Deer Stalking $100.00-125.00
Eagle $650.00-700.00
"Cricket" $125.00-150.00
#4 - Two Hunters $125.00-150.00
"Attention..." $125.00-150.00
"The Butterfly" $125.00-150.00
"Flowers Of Literature" $125.00-150.00
#5 - "The Foxglove" .. $125.00-150.00
"Actors" $125.00-150.00
"Teaching Tray.." $125.00-150.00

Page 14
#6 - "Peg In The Ring" $125.00-150.00
The Swing $125.00-150.00
"Northern Spell" $125.00-150.00
Blind Man's Bluff $125.00-150.00
"He Thast ..." $125.00-150.00
#7 - Boy & Pie $125.00-150.00
Girl & Soldier $150.00-175.00
Two Soldiers $150.00-175.00
Boys In A Fight $100.00-125.00
Pig Feeding $125.00-150.00
#8 - Prosper Freedom $475.00-525.00
Girl & Soldier $150.00-175.00
Two Hunters $125.00-175.00
Single Hunter $125.00-175.00

Page 15
#9 - "Emma" $125.00-175.00
"A Gift For Hanna" $175.00-200.00
"Henry" $125.00-175.00
"Maria" $175.00-200.00
#10 - "Eliza" $175.00-200.00
"Dorothy" $175.00-200.00
"Susan" $175.00-200.00
"Frederick" $175.00-200.00
#11 - "A Mother's
    Affection"............. $150.00-200.00
The Seasons $150.00-200.00
"That Jack Built" $150.00-200.00
"The World Expects.." $150.00-200.00
#12 - "Bless the..." $350.00-450.00
"Reward Of Merit $200.00-275.00
"Present For Boy"....... $175.00-200.00
"For Loving A Book" . $150.00-200.00
#13 - Poppy $400.00-600.00
"A Trifle For Margaret" $400.00-500.00
"Present For Girl" $350.00-450.00
"For My Favorite Girl" $250.00-350.00
Ropes Of Luster $300.00-375.00
"A Dog For Robert" ... $350.00-375.00
Lafayette-Washington
    (black) $1,500.00-2,000.00
    (red) $1,800.00-2,000.00
Lady, Basket & Dog .. $300.00-400.00

Page 17
#14 - Lady Feeding
    Hens $150.00-175.00
The Judge $150.00-175.00
Franklin Maxim $175.00-250.00
"A, B, C" Mug $175.00-200.00
#15 - Nursery Rhyme
    Egg Cup $30.00-40.00
Staffordshire Cps/Scrs ..ea.$50.00-75.00

Merry Christmas
    Cps./Scrs. .... ea. $100.00-125.00
Cheap Shop $200.00-275.00
Poor Richard $150.00-175.00
Sloth Like Rust $150.00-175.00
Debts $150.00-175.00
Gains Without Pains ... $150.00-175.00

Page 18
#16 - "VWX" $150.00-175.00
"Feeding The Chickens" $150.00-175.00
"Horse" $150.00-175.00
" An Idle Man" $150.00-175.00
#17 - "K" Is For Kitten $200.00-275.00
"N" & "O" With Owl . $200.00-275.00
"P" Parrot $200.00-275.00
"T" Lady & Boy $200.00-275.00
"X" Lady, &"W"
    Christ $275.00-300.00
#18 - Fishing Party $150.00-175.00
Children Shooting Bow $150.00-175.00
The Boar Hunt $85.00-100.00
"H" Horse Whose Paces; & "G"
    For Gander $175.00-200.00

Page 19
#19 - "B" Is For Ball; "A" Stands
    For Apple $200.00-275.00
"D" Dash; "C" Cat $200.00-275.00
"M N O" Whip Top $200.00-275.00
"F" For Fox & "E" For
    Elephant $200.00-275.00
"H" With Horse & "G"
    with Gander $200.00-275.00
#20 - Stripes $200.00-250.00
Alphabet $200.00-275.00
Sponge $150.00-175.00
Pink Luster Floral $200.00-250.00
Person With Burden ... $200.00-300.00
Wagon Wheel $200.00-300.00
Criss-Crossing $200.00-300.00

Page 20
#21 - Spiral Shell $275.00-300.00
Blue Bells $275.00-300.00
Floral Overlap $175.00-200.00
Fan $200.00-275.00
Lustered Bird $275.00-300.00
Lunch Boxes $125.00-175.00
Tin Mugs $300.00-375.00
#22 - Bird $150.00-175.00
Alphabet $125.00-150.00
Fox & Goose $100.00-125.00
Alphabet $125.00-150.00

Page 21
#23 - German Whistle Mug
    (Hamilton) $100.00-125.00
#24 - Frances Alden $75.00-100.00
#25 - Kate Greenaway . $75.00-100.00
Alice In Wonderland, &
    Mad Hatter's Tea $75.00-100.00

Page 22 - CHILDREN'S CHINA PLATES

China Plates #1 -
ABCD Bird $70.00-80.00
#2 -"By The Plough..." $150.00-250.00
Oriental $150.00-250.00
"Benevolence..." $150.00-250.00
Farming Plates $150.00-200.00

Page 23
#3 - Mischievious Cat . $150.00-200.00
Old Mother Hubbard .. $150.00-200.00
"Frolics Of Youth.." ... $150.00-200.00
The Blacksmith $150.00-200.00
#4 - Soldiers $200.00-225.00
Docteur $100.00-125.00

Two People $200.00-250.00
Child & Bird $150.00-175.00

Page 24
#5 - "Sacred History of Joseph and His
    Brethren" ... (set) $800.00-1,000.00
#25 -"Now I Have A Cow" $175.00-190.00
Children & Train $175.00-190.00
"Experience Keeps.." ... $175.00-190.00
Tiger, Kangaroo $175.00-190.00
On The River Bank $175.00-190.00

Page 25 - SAUCERS, TUMBLERS, PLATES & BOWLS

Royal Doulton Plates

Royal Doulton #1 -
Nursery Tales Variety -
    Tumbler $85.00-100.00
    Mug $65.00-90.00
    Plates .... ea. $65.00-90.00
    Cup & Saucer $90.00-125.00
#2 - "My Pretty Maid"ea. $75.00-125.00
#3 - Mother Goose Plateea $60.00-90.00
    Cup & Saucer $90.00-125.00
    Tumbler $85.00-125.00
#4 - Ride A Cock Horse
    Plates .... ea. $75.00-125.00
    Pitcher $75.00-125.00
#5 - Little Miss Muffet
    Glass $68.00-90.00
#6 - Hey Diddle Diddle,
    Cup & Saucer $90.00-125.00
    Tumbler $85.00-100.00
    Plate $75.00-100.00
#7 - Old Mother Hubbard Cup &
    Saucer $90.00-125.00
#8 - Little Bo Peep Plates $75.00-125.00

Page 27
#9 - "There Was A Little Man."
    Mug $75.00-100.00
    Plate $75.00-100.00
    Cup & Saucer $90.00-110.00
    Bowl $75.00-100.00
#10 - Queen Of Hearts
    Plates .... ea. $75.00-100.00
To Market To Market ... $75.00-100.00
Mary Quite Contrary ... $75.00-100.00
#11 - Little Tom Tucker
    Plates $75.00-100.00

Page 28 - BEVERAGE CHINA SETS IN CHINA

Beverage Set #1 -
Greenaway Basket &
    Jugs $750.00-900.00
#2 - Beer Set $200.00-275.00
#3 - Bavarian Stein Set .. $35.00-45.00

Page 29 - TEA SETS & DINNER SETS
Creamware ...... set $3,000.00-3,500.00
Leed's Floral $850.00-1,000.00
Cherry Tree $475.00-800.00

Page 30
London Shape $1,000.00-1,200.00
Adam Buck $3,500.00-4,000.00
Rogers Blue & White . $600.00-800.00

Page 31
Wind Flower $2,500.00-2,800.00
Meigh's Moss Rose . $900.00-1,800.00
    Dinner Set $1,200.00-2,500.00

Page 32
Dimmocks Blue Band . $475.00-600.00
    Dinner Set $800.00-1,500.00
Godwin No. 26 .... $525.00-625.00

Page 49
Davenport's Pink Luster

Blossoms $1,200.00-2,200.00
Columbia Star $2,500.00-3,000.00
Sprig Tea Set $475.00-700.00
    Dinner Set $900.00-1,800.00

Page 50
Barrow & Co. $550.00-675.00
    Sponge Design . $1,000.00-1,800.00
Double Bands $275.00-400.00

Page 51
Amherst Japan
    Tea Set $2,000.00-2,500.00
    Dinner Set 3,000.00-3,500.00
Green & White Seaweed$500.00-800.00
Trellis $350.00-475.00
Matlock $350.00-475.00

Page 52
Plain Pink Bands $375.00-425.00
Split Handle $375.00-575.00
Chintz $300.00-375.00
Phone $125.00-150.00

Page 53
Gold Clover Leaf $375.00-425.00
Pompadore $300.00-350.00
Paneled Willow $350.00-375.00

Page 54
English Blue Willow .. $350.00-375.00
Octagon Blue Willow . $400.00-500.00
Spatterware $425.00-600.00
Stick Spatterware $375.00-450.00

Page 55
Apple Blossom $250.00-350.00
Persian $400.00-600.00

Page 56
Derby White & Gold .. $850.00-950.00
Pink Ovals/Diamonds . $275.00-300.00
Cream/Brown Flowers $450.00-475.00
Rib-Moulded Pk/Wh ... $325.00-350.00

Page 57
Shell-Thin/Violets $775.00-825.00
Luster Trimmed
    Flowers $175.00-225.00

ENGLISH TEA SETS, PEOPLE, ANIMALS
Children's Pastimes $800.00-900.00
At The Well $475.00-525.00

Page 58
Gipsey $575.00-625.00
Oriental Youth $800.00-1,000.00
Girl With A Goat...(depending on color
    treatment) $450.00-925.00

Page 59
Italian $450.00-550.00
Woman By The Urn ... $550.00-750.00
The Bower $500.00-850.00

Page 60
Farm $425.00-600.00
Chang $350.00-525.00
Brown Willow $225.00-275.00

Page 61
Birds & Holly $750.00-900.00
Stag $200.00-275.00
Mae With Apron $250.00-375.00
Bye-Bye Bunting $425.00-500.00

Page 62
Bye-Baby $300.00-385.00
To Market! To Market!$350.00-375.00
Ivanhoe $325.00-375.00

Page 63
English Dutch Pots $325.00-375.00
Novelty Toby $125.00-185.00

ENGLISH DINNER & DESSERT SETS
Lion's Heads $3,500.00-4,500.00

Page 64
Brown Banded $2,000.00-3,000.00
Ferns & Flowers $800.00-1,000.00
Blue Willow $2,500.00-3,000.00
Wood's Willow $2,800.00-3,000.00
Page 65
Laurel Leaves $800.00-1,800.00
English Scenes $3,500.00-6,000.00
Tower $3,000.00-4,000.00
Page 66
Monopteros $4,200.00-4,800.00
Blue Willow $3,800.00-4,000.00
Monastery Hill $3,000.00-3,800.00
Page 67
English Oriental $2,000.00-2,500.00
Garden Sports Tea
Set $1,000.00-1,200.00
Dinner Set $1,500.00-2,000.00
Copper Luster Leaf $2,800.00-3,500.00
Page 68
Asiatic Birds
reg. colors $2,500.00-3,000.00
flow blue 3,000.00-4,000.00
Slant Stripe Border $1,500.00-1,800.00
Page 69
Myrtle Wreath $1,500.00-1,800.00
Calico $475.00-600.00
Chelsea Pattern $750.00-850.00
Leaf Border in Mulberry $375.00-400.00
Page 70
Green Loops $900.00-1,500.00
Amadeus $500.00-800.00
Delicate Seaweed $900.00-1,500.00
Page 71
Child's Variety $425.00-900.00
Bur & Blossom $800.00-975.00
Fishers $900.00-1,500.00
Page 72
Copeland Blue & Gold $300.00-600.00
Floral Staffordshire $375.00-650.00
Chinese Red/Cobalt $3,000.00-3,500.00
Pearl Dessert
Dessert $1,000.00-1,275.00
Dinner Set $1,500.00-3,000.00
Page 73
Fruit & Dessert Set $475.00-500.00
Blue Willow $800.00-1,200.00
Black Willow $1,000.00-1,500.00
Blue Daisy $300.00-375.00
Page 74
Chintz $375.00-450.00
Rosamond $800.00-900.00
Bishop Blue Willow ... $400.00-450.00
Page 75
Bishop Children $375.00-425.00
Shell Ware Willow $200.00-250.00
Patchwork $375.00-400.00
Rhodesia $1,000.00-1,500.00
Page 76
Humphrey's Clock-
Tea Set $600.00-675.00
Dinner Set $675.00-775.00
Tea & Dinner Set ... $650.00-950.00
Dessert Set $1,200.00-1,500.00
Page 77
Storks $275.00-325.00
GERMAN TEA SETS, FLOWERS, BANDS & SCENIC STRUCTURES
Applied Flowers $375.00-500.00
Floral Cabaret Set $700.00-1,000.00
Indigo Flowers $1,500.00-2,200.00
Page 78
Footed RS Prussia . $1,200.00-1,500.00
Scales $375.00-400.00
Pink Luster $200.00-275.00
Scenic Structures $375.00-425.00
Page 79
German Holly $400.00-500.00
Rose Bud $200.00-250.00
Fuchsia Enameled $400.00-500.00
Bent Bud $200.00-250.00
Page 80
Blue Elegance $200.00-275.00
Hearts With Stars $200.00-275.00
Gold With Pink Roses $200.00-250.00
Petite Christmas Holly $375.00-400.00
Page 81
Peach Roses With
Gold $125.00-175.00
Cobalt Berolina $175.00-200.00
Tete-A-Tete $375.00-400.00
Silver/Orange On White $125.00-150.00
Page 82
Butterflies & Flowers . $150.00-190.00
GERMAN TEA SETS, CHILDREN, ANIMALS AND NURSERY TALES
Christmas $375.00-400.00
German Christmas $500.00-700.00
Sledding Home $500.00-600.00
Page 83
Angel & Star $600.00-700.00
Victorian Ladies $425.00-525.00
Page 84
Snowman & Children . $450.00-575.00
Dutch People $400.00-425.00
Florence $425.00-525.00
Page 85
Cats' Thanksgiving $475.00-575.00
Clown/Animal on Pigs $475.00-575.00
German Circus $475.00-575.00
Quaggy Duck (mint) $250.00
Quaggy Duck (poor) $200.00
5½" Clown $200.00
8½" Clown $300.00
"Kiki" $150.00-250.00
Velvet Boar $100.00
Page 86
Children's Frolic $475.00-575.00
Girls With Bear $675.00-800.00
Rain Storm $400.00-500.00
RS Portrait Scenes $1,200.00-2,000.00
Page 87
Royal Bayreuth Scenes $600.00-900.00
Sunbonnet Babies . $1,000.00-1,800.00
Page 88
Housekeeping $450.00-550.00
White/White Animals . $400.00-500.00
Circus Tricks $400.00-500.00
Page 89
Cat Band $400.00-575.00
At The Circus $275.00-375.00
Tease A Kitten $400.00-500.00
Page 90
Driving Anmals $375.00-500.00
Cupid $225.00-400.00
Ethnic Group $1,800.00-2,200.00
Indians $1,000.00-1,800.00
Page 91
Romantic $500.00-700.00
GERMAN DINNER & HOUSEKEEPING SETS
Feldblumen $425.00-500.00
Oyster Stew Set $400.00-450.00
Page 92
Elegant Pink Roses $490.00-525.00
Chowder Set $475.00-550.00
Marked RS Set . $1,800.00-2,400.00
Red Roses $350.00-450.00
FRENCH TEA SETS
Paris Scenic $400.00-500.00
Page 93
Gothic $300.00-400.00
Soft Blue With Gold ... $325.00-400.00
French Packaging . $1,800.00-2,500.00
Page 94
French Coffee Set $225.00-250.00
French Floral $175.00-250.00
Bonne Nuit $175.00-200.00
Page 95
French Boys & Girls ... $200.00-250.00
Violets On Soft Paste .. $150.00-175.00
FRENCH DINNER SETS
French Children $1,200.00-1,500.00
Page 96
French Stencils $375.00-400.00
French-In-The-Box $600.00-800.00
Forget-Me-Nots &
Pink Trim $375.00-400.00
Page 97 - AMERICAN TEA & DINNER SETS
Blue Spongware $900.00-1,000.00
Ironstone with Flowers $125.00-150.00
Robin Red Breast $675.00-800.00
Page 98
Rocky $175.00-225.00
Cinderella & The Prince $375.00-475.00
Page 100
Kate Greenaway Illus. $580.00-800.00
Floral $125.00-150.00
Children & Dachshund $500.00-600.00
Page 101
Kate Greenaway -
Tea Set $475.00-575.00
Dinner Set $475.00-600.00
Greenaway Dinner Set $500.00-800.00
Page 102 - JAPANESE TEA & DINNER SETS
Azalea $2,200.00-2,400.00
Different Designs ... $125.00-200.00
American Flag $200.00-300.00
Birthday Party $200.00-300.00
Page 103
Silhouettes $200.00-300.00
Floral $575.00-650.00
Sports Minded Bears & Steiff Animals
Good Condition $500.00-600.00
17" Rico Rabbit $400.00
without Skis & Poles $200.00
"Zolac" $500.00
Page 104 - JAPANESE BLUE WILLOW
Creamers: 2", 1½" $25.00-35.00
Sugars: 2", 2¾" $35.00-45.00
Cups: 1½", 1⅛" $15.00-20.00
Saucers: 3¾", 3⅜" $15.00-20.00
Plates: 5", 4⅜", 3¾" $10.00-20.00
Cake Plates: 5¼", 4¼" $100.00-125.00
Blue Plate Specials: 5", 4¼" $60.00-80.00
Veg. Bowl: 5⅜" $60.00-80.00
Tureens: 4", 4½" $60.00-80.00
Teapots: 3¾" 2⅝" $50.00-80.00
Sauce Boats: $60.00-80.00
Open-Handled Cake
Plates .... ea. $100.00-125.00
Soup or Berry Bowls . ea. $40.00-60.00
Grill Plates .... ea. $60.00-80.00
Veg. Bowl $60.00-80.00
Covered Dishes $60.00-80.00
Gravy Boats .... ea. $60.00-80.00
Page 105 - Top Row:
Unusual Teapots ..... ea. $75.00-125.00
Second Row:
Reed Handled .... ea. $125.00-150.00
Sets With Teapots $350.00-425.00
Third Row:
Flat-sided Teapots .... ea. $75.00-125.00
Set $275.00-350.00
Largest Teapot Set $225.00-350.00
Oval Teapot Set $150.00-250.00
Bottom Row:
Tea Set $250.00-290.00
EUROPEAN TEA SETS
Scenic Pink Luster $300.00-375.00
Russian Tea Set $275.00-400.00
THE PLAYHOUSE KITCHEN
Page 107 - Kitchen Ware
Kitchen #1 -
Pewter Tea Set $375.00-450.00
#2 - Pewter Tea Set $350.00-450.00
#3 - Silverplate Tea $450.00-675.00
Page 108
#4 -Doll-Sized Silver .. $250.00-400.00
#5 -Housekeeping Pot . $300.00-475.00
#6 -Brass Tea Kettle & Coffee
Pot $375.00-475.00
Page 109
#7 - Cherry & Floral Tea
Sets .... ea. $700.00-775.00
Bear $1,000.00-1,200.00
Vase $200.00-300.00
#8 - Cobalt Granite $500.00-575.00
Page 110
#9 - Utility Rack &
Spoons $700.00-800.00
Krumcake Skillet $150.00-250.00
Spotted Pan $100.00-125.00
Bl/Wh Two-Handled Pan $75.00-100.00
Long-Handled Pan $75.00-125.00
Wash Pan $40.00-75.00
Pie Spade $100.00-150.00
Funnel $40.00-80.00
Creamer $40.00-60.00
Blue Mug $10.00-30.00
Packaged Flatware $40.00-90.00
Speckled Tea Set $225.00-400.00
Blue Spoons .... ea. $20.00-60.00
Writing Box $125.00-150.00
Bear $1,000.00-1,200.00
Page 111
#10 - Enamel Ware Stew
Sets $800.00-900.00
Page 112
#11 - Pewter Flatware .. **set $300.00-350.00**
#12 - Bl./Wh. Handled Knife, Fork
& Spoon **(place set.) $60.00-100.00**
Bone Handled Knife
& Fork .... **(place set.) $60.00-75.00**
Pewter Knife, Fork, Spoon,
Knife Rest, Napkin Ring
(place set.) $12.00-15.00
20th Cent. Metal, Knife, Fork,
Spoon, (set for 4) $10.00-15.00
Salt Dips .... ea. $12.00-15.00
A Napkin Ring Holder-
Silver/Pewter $10.00-15.00
Unknown Metal ...... ea. $2.00-10.00
Kitchen Utensils .... ea. $3.00-5.00
Page 113
#13 - "Like Mother's" $175.00-190.00
#14 - Flatware Roll $60.00-75.00
#15 - Miniature Table Service
Set $275.00-400.00
Page 114
#16 - Bird & Nest $40.00-50.00
#17 - Gray Granite
Pots/Pans set $130.00-160.00

#18 - White Granite
Pots/Pans set $125.00-150.00

Page 115

#19 - Revere Ware $150.00-175.00

#20 - Kitchen Equipment

4¾" Warming Dish $35.00-75.00

5" Cookie Jar $75.00-150.00

Coffee Grinder $150.00-175.00

Cooking Pots $150.00-175.00

Hunter's Toy Sifter $100.00-175.00

Page 116

#21 - Glass Jar &

Beater $20.00-50.00

Waffle Iron $120.00-200.00

Weller Crock &

Beater $250.00-350.00

METAL, GLASS, CROCKERY & WOOD

#22 -

Green Crock $35.00-100.00

Bl/Wh Crock & Bail $50.00-100.00

Kraut Crock $40.00-100.00

Brown Slip/Cream Exterior $60.00-125.00

Yellow Ware Bowl $50.00-100.00

Potato Masher $40.00-75.00

Nest Yellow Ware $250.00-375.00

Sweetheart Bowl $200.00-250.00

Brown Slip Bowl $50.00-100.00

Page 117

#23 - Stone Ware Jugs

White/Blue Bands $50.00-100.00

Flat-sided Flask Jug . $50.00-100.00

Tall Brown Jugs $40.00-100.00

Bennington Pitcher .. $60.00-100.00

Gray Whiskey Jug ... $50.00-100.00

Brown Cider Jug $40.00-100.00

#24 - Buckets, Pins & Cans

Sugar Bucket $80.00-175.00

Cocoa Tin $65.00-100.00

Bucket $60.00-100.00

Bucket $40.00-100.00

Rolling Pin $40.00-75.00

#25 - Miscellaneous Crocks

First & Last $40.00-75.00

Center $30.00-90.00

Page 118

#26 - Butter Moulds & Prints

Star Mould $100.00-150.00

Cow Print $250.00-350.00

Leaf Mould $200.00-300.00

Acorn Mould $150.00-250.00

Acorn Print $125.00-175.00

Flower Mould $150.00-200.00

#27 - Miniature Baskets

Clothes Basket $175.00-200.00

Melon Basket $175.00-275.00

Market Basket $175.00-275.00

Butt or Gizzard $300.00-400.00

3 Descending Butt or Gizzard

Baskets .... ea. $200.00-300.00

Basket With Egg $125.00-175.00

Egg $40.00-75.00

Market Basket $175.00-225.00

#27a - Picnic Basket .. $225.00-300.00

#28 - Misc. Toy Products

Scale $60.00-75.00

Royal Gas Stove $125.00-175.00

Pearl Iron $125.00-200.00

Tin Lunch Box $40.00-75.00

Sugar Scoop $20.00-60.00

Tin Salt Box $90.00-100.00

Covered Cup $30.00-75.00

Washboard $75.00-125.00

#29 - Coffee Grinder .. $125.00-150.00

Wall Coffee Grinder ... $150.00-200.00

Russian Urn $75.00-100.00

Tin Canister/Cereal Set ... $60.00-75.00

Brass Krumcake Skillet .. $30.00-40.00

Funnel Blue & White $10.00-30.00

Wooden Flatware Tray . $75.00-100.00

Page 120

#30 - Sugar Box $125.00-150.00

#31 - Castor Set $200.00-250.00

#32 - Coffee Grinder . $175.00-200.00

#33 - Coffee Grinder . $175.00-200.00

Page 121

#34 - Toy Coffee Maker $40.00-60.00

#35 - Stoves

Tin/Cast Iron Stove . $375.00-500.00

Baby $225.00-300.00

Tea Kettle $60.00-90.00

Food Grinder $20.00-30.00

Cooking Pot & Bucket $40.00-50.00

#36 - Small Stoves

Royal $60.00-150.00

Royal $75.00-150.00

Kent $125.00-175.00

Eagle $125.00-175.00

Williams $75.00-125.00

Geneva Champion $75.00-100.00

Daisy $75.00-125.00

Kilgore $80.00-150.00

Page 122

#37 - Patty Pans $5.00-10.00

Bumpy Fruit Mould .. ea. $10.00-15.00

Strawberry Mould $10.00-15.00

Copper Mould $40.00-75.00

Toast Rack $20.00-30.00

#38 - Blue Housekeeping

Set $600.00-800.00

Page 123

#39 - Colander $400.00-550.00

#40 - Blue Granite Ware

Pie Spade $100.00-150.00

Dippers $75.00-100.00

Strainer $60.00-100.00

Grater $100.00-200.00

Salt Box $250.00-350.00

Tea Kettle $500.00-675.00

#41 - Blue Tea Set $450.00-575.00

Page 124

#42 - Blue Enamel Tea $300.00-475.00

Steiff Lamb $125.00-175.00

#43 - Wash Pan/Pail ea. $375.00-475.00

#44 - Lenci Doll $500.00-675.00

Spoon Holder $275.00-375.00

Flour Bin $375.00-400.00

Utensil Rack $200.00-250.00

Page 125

#45 - Weller Set $350.00-425.00

Food Savers $250.00-275.00

1950s Mixer $40.00-75.00

"Teddy Li" $475.00-500.00

#46 - Cereal Set $275.00-300.00

Sunbeam Mixer $200.00-250.00

Page 126

#47 - Utensils .... ea. $25.00-35.00

#48 - Cleaning Equip. $35.00-45.00

Sample Cleaners .... ea. $25.00-35.00

Brush Set $45.00-55.00

Big-Footed Bear $300.00-375.00

Page 127

#49 - "Brushes Like

Mothers" $50.00-75.00

#50 - Dish Washing Set . $85.00-90.00

Bear $425.00-475.00

Page 128

#51 - Corner Grocer .. $500.00-675.00

#52 - Food Samples . ea. $45.00-55.00

Page 129

#53 - Coffee Samples ea. $45.00-65.00

Wall Coffee Grinder ... $200.00-225.00

Table Coffee Grinder .. $150.00-175.00

#54 - Bear On A Picnic

Bear $600.00-1,000.00

Basket $175.00-200.00

Spoons $50.00-60.00

Creamer $40.00-50.00

Sapphire Tumble Up $175.00-200.00

Bowl $40.00-50.00

Page 130

#55 - Bear $1,800.00-2,300.00

Picnic Basket $225.00-300.00

Beer Sample $9.00-15.00

#56 - Sand Toys $275.00-325.00

Yellow Bear $400.00-600.00

#57 - Place Card Holder $75.00-85.00

Page 131

#58 - Red Ware Churn $500.00-800.00

Rolling Pin $45.00-125.00

KITCHEN FURNITURE

#59 - Table & Chairs $1,500.00-2,000.00

Page 132

#60 - Water Bench $1,200.00-2,000.00

#61 - Majestic Stove $4,000.00-10,000.00

Bucket & Shovel $70.00-125.00

Roasting Pan $30.00-75.00

Tea Kettle $75.00-100.00

Waffle Iron $75.00-150.00

Brass Coffee Pots .. ea. $100.00-125.00

Granite Coffee Pot $225.00-375.00

Page 133

#62 - Cupboard $900.00-1,200.00

Dog $75.00-125.00

#63 - Ice Box $500.00-800.00

Ice Cream Freezer $150.00-200.00

#64 - Cupboard $1,800.00-2,200.00

China Spice Set $200.00-325.00

Sample Fruit Jars ...... ea. $12.00-20.00

Page 134

#65 - Bucks Jr. Stoves

Tea Kettles .... ea. $60.00-125.00

Bear $300.00-400.00

Stove $800.00-1,500.00

2nd Stove $300.00-900.00

Toy Iron $40.00-70.00

#66 - New England Kitchen

Stove $700.00-1,500.00

Waffle Iron $150.00-250.00

#67 - Tappan Stove $2,500.00-3,500.00

Shovel, Bucket ...... ea. $125.00-200.00

Tea Kettle $500.00-675.00

Covered Pan $400.00-600.00

3 Skillets On Wall . ea. $175.00-225.00

Page 135

#68 - Hide Chair .. $1,000.00-1,800.00

#69 - Dry Sink $1,500.00-2,000.00

#70 - Cupboard $3,000.00-3,500.00

Page 136

#71 - Pie Safe $1,000.00-1,800.00

#72 - Ice Box $800.00-1,000.00

THE PLAYHOUSE DINING ROOM

Page 137 - Dining Room Furniture

Dining Room #1 -

Sideboard $1,500.00-2,000.00

Willow Tea Ware .. set $300.00-385.00

#2 - Revival Side-

board $1,200.00-2,000.00

Page 138

#3 - Cupboard $3,000.00-3,500.00

Cherry Framed Mirror...$300.00-350.00

#4 - Dumb Waiter $350.00-475.00

Page 139

#5 - .... $15,000.00 & up

#6 - Sideboard $2,000.00-2,500.00

Lusters $600.00-800.00

THE PLAYHOUSE PARLOR

Page 140 - Parlor Furniture & Access.

Parlor Furniture #1 -

Chair $3,000.00-3,800.00

#2 - Automata $7,000.00-15,000.00

#3 - Piano & Bench ... $600.00-900.00

Page 141

#4 - Grand Piano $275.00-300.00

#5 - Player Piano $425.00-500.00

#6 - Fern Stand $200.00-225.00

#7 - French Tea Stand $800.00-1,000.00

Page 142

#8 - Muffin Stand $150.00-275.00

#9 - Brownie Frame $75.00-125.00

#10 - Toy Frames ...... ea. $50.00-75.00

Page 143

#11 - Lithophane $200.00-250.00

#12 - Lincoln

Rocker $1,000.00-2,800.00

Night Stand $1,200.00-2,000.00

English China ..... set $900.00-1,000.00

THE PLAYHOUSE LIBRARY

Page 144 - Library Furniture

& Writing Equipage

Library #1 -

Wooton Desk $18,000.00-25,000.00

#2 - Secretary $2,500.00-3,000.00

#3 - Oak Roll Curtain

Desk $800.00-1,800.00

#4 - Canterbury $1,500.00-1,800.00

#5 - Albums .... ea. $150.00-200.00

Bookcase Book Ends .. $200.00-225.00

Leather Ink Well & Feather $300.00-375.00

Diaries, Dict., Bibles . ea. $50.00-75.00

Page 146

#6 - Book Filled Rack $200.00-275.00

Silver Writing Set $375.00-475.00

#7 - Pewter Desk Set . $475.00-575.00

#8 - Suitcase Desk $1,000.00-1,500.00

Lap Desk $150.00-200.00

China Ink Well Set $85.00-100.00

Sterling Ink Well $50.00-100.00

English Lap Desk $125.00-200.00

Slate-Slant $400.00-500.00

Ink Box $175.00-200.00

Page 147

#9 - Portable Desk $475.00-900.00

#10 - Desk Set $1,500.00-1,800.00

THE PLAYHOUSE BEDROOM & GROOMING EQUIPMENT

Page 148 - Bedroom Furniture

Bedroom #1 -

Oak Washstand $1,000.00-1,500.00

Chamber Set $375.00-525.00

#2 - Fainting Couch $2,000.00-2,800.00

#3 - Fainting Couch . $800.00-1,000.00

Page 149

#4 - Mule Chest ... $2,000.00-3,500.00

#5 - Empire Chest ... $800.00-1,800.00

#6 - Tramp Art Chest . $400.00-475.00

#7 - Tramp Art

Dresser $450.00-575.00

Page 150

#8 - Walnut What-Not $500.00-600.00

Victorian Purses .... ea. $90.00-100.00

Larkin Desk $700.00-800.00

Brass Hat Rack $175.00-275.00

Table of Contents

Introduction

If a cartographer created a map of the intriguing world of the playhouse and its equipage, the map would include sunny peaks of exquisite taste and elegance as well as shadowed valleys of slip-shod workmanship. There would be caves of mystery filled with strange and unclaimed designs. Exposed clay strata and glaze would reveal secret techniques of the past. The rosy-cosy harbors of the nurseries and playhouses would reflect the niceties of life's comforts and security, indicating in tandem the manner of life in the "big house." Nearly everything made for Mother was in turn produced in miniature form for the little hostess.

Through this book we can enjoy, as collectors, a second childhood. We can sail the sea of examples puzzling over the delicate incongruities rendered by the adults who created the great toy movement. These adults recede into a paper doll status while the child and the play-pretties spring to the forefront to be examined and marveled over. The scenario of youth can be rerun through this book to find out what it is that makes us smile...what it is that compels us to collect.

When raindrops pelt the windows like handfuls of berries, we collectors enjoy cuddling-up with a book dealing with our favorite subjects. This tea-cozy moment is an escape into pleasant research which allows us to peek into a time regarded as gentler, more refined. Even though this is not a realistic picture, it serves the purpose of the moment . . . escape. In reality, we are the fortunate ones living in a fusion of old and new; the ones living in the perfect moment in history. We can yo-yo from then to now enjoying the work of the masters in the comfort of our homes; shop for their ware in the convenience of perfectly controlled vehicles; and sleep over in the inns of the past which are redone to accommodate the spoiled and pampered. We are allowed to tramp or tiptoe through history according to our conveniece forgetting as we please ourselves about the unpleasantness that often occurred in order to produce the products with which we are so enamored.

Now, once more, the past is awakened and examined. The charm-control that children have always had over adults is once more in evidence as hundreds of child-pleasing toy products are carefully placed in displays of honor in the homes of collectors and in books such as this so that their history may be reviewed, enjoyed and most importantly, remembered.

As our ears meet the shattering din of stereos and the jangle of telephones, we glance quickly at the never bothersome children parading in giddy relief around the china and glass sets. The cacophony ends and quiet as a swan's feather we are "tessered" to a Greenaway time, a peaceful time . . . a you and me time.

> Do you recall the dimity design
> That was on a china set of mine?
> We had camomile tea in tiny cups,
> A small glass plate on which to sup',
> A few friends to share the grace--
> The strawberry forks in just the right place.
>
> I'm calling your memories one more time.
> Humphrey's Clock gives one last chime,
> We've a quiet time for remembering at last . . .
> A wrinkle in time into the past.

Doris Anderson Lechler

Collecting Toy China

My first book, *Children's Glass Dishes*, published by Thomas Nelson, was mainly concerned with American children's toy glassware. The second book, *Children's Glass Dishes, China and Furniture*, published by Collector Books, expanded the field to include children's china (mostly German) and toy furniture, both American and European. This book ventures even further into the playhouse, investigating English toy china and other playhouse equipage used by the little hostess and amassed by collectors of today.

In this publication, when china pattern names are marked on the ware, this name will be acknowledged by "correct name" after the title. In other cases, when toy china is described, a name will be given the set which best describes the design found on that particular set of blanks. This naming is an aid to collectors and dealers during buying, selling and cataloguing.

Measurements are given when possible including the height for everything except saucers, plates and other things calling for diameter readings. (At times, some articles will have even more in-depth measurements.)

References to other books are given by stating the name of the author(s), title and page number.

The prices are listed with the pertinent data for convenience of the collector, dealer, author and publisher. These prices are usually set by the owners of the items shown in the publication. These owners are qualified because they are advanced collectors, dealers or researchers who are in tune with the reality of current market trends and values on both ends of the spectrum . . .buying and selling. A range of prices, in most cases, will be given to accommodate regional differences.

One must bear in mind that all items in this book were meant for play rather than for collecting and that prices are for the ware in the best possible condition and as complete as possible. One must not expect mint products each time there is a buying occasion or one will be disappointed as well as frustrated. Collecting children's china is an enjoyable adventure which is spreading across the world. Those who seem the happiest in the collecting endeavor are the ones who have escaped "snobamania". These happy collectors realize that no one person can own it all. Where would they put it? They know, too, that no one person can know it all. The collectors who find joy in their discoveries as well as other people's are those who are satisfied with their collecting methods and their classification selection. They feed this satisfaction by finding items for themselves as well as by helping others find additions for their collections. These collectors are also willing to impart information to the ever growing field of finders.

There is no place in toy collecting for the words "always" and "never". It is well known among members of the knowledgeable group of collectors that producers of toys of the past did not place much emphasis on cataloguing, perfecting, or instructing their customers. They were in a very competitive business, therefore, they produced the products, sold them as quickly and efficiently as possible, and moved on to other matters . . . an untidy procedure with interesting results meant only to be enjoyed.

Those who may be afflicted by a mania for attributions will be uncomfortable in the toy glass and toy china fields because discoveries are popping up each day, only to be shot down the following week. Ruth Webb Lee, in her SANDWICH GLASS book wrote: "It is an exceptional collector who prefers to own a fine work of art, 'Artist Unknown' rather than an inferior piece to which a famous signature may be attached. The blue ribbon of an attribution is nothing to be either sure of or proud of, unless it hangs on a really fine work. Our collectors were too long the victims of our national ailment--labelitis Americana--which is a near blood relation of our fondness for slogans."

You will find, therefore, in this book, as in the second book, words such as "unknown origin" and "date in question" as well as pictures of toys which have limited information. The importance of a book such as this is to show toys from the past which may still be collected. These are toys which were produced for play and sold to middle and upper classes families. The items in this book from the Strong Museum are shown here, not because they are unique, but because they are not. Margaret Woodbury Strong collected middle class accouterments, the likes of which are available to collectors of today. Her "museum of delight" in Rochester, New York, features great attractions which inspire collecting rather than defeat it.

Those of you who have an eye for fine paintings and can tell from the work of art who painted it, may use some of the same criterion for recognizing the work of potters. There are, however, the same forecasting problems. Just as in fine paintings, there were those who emulated the master potters, producing work so close to the "real thing" that it is difficult to tell exactly which pottery originated the product. The masters shared in the painting world, just as they did in the potting world--sometimes on purpose and at other times without knowing that the best form of flattery had been applied to their particular contributions.

Early Mugs and Plates

The early china mugs and plates are from an outstanding private collection whose owners wish to convey the fact that condition of plates and mugs is a very important factor in pricing this ware.

Descriptions for each picture grouping will be explained from left to right. The measurements indicate mug height and plate diameter.

* indicates the item may also be seen in the color section or on the covers.

Mugs #1 Search The Scriptures, Holy Bible, floral, 2¹/₂″. Price range: $65.00 to 85.00; The Path Of Truth is Plain and Safe, Holy Bible, 2⁵/₈″. Price range: $65.00 to 85.00; Faith, shows a person with the cross, lustered rim, 2³/₈″. Price range: $75.00 to 90.00.

Mugs #2 Cat In A Bonnet With Glasses, yellow and green on tan; 2³/₈″. Price range: $55.00 to 68.00; Cats At Play, colored transfer, 2³/₄″. Price range: $55.00 to 68.00; Cat Accident, knocking over a table, 2⁵/₈″. Price range: $55.00 to 68.00; Boy and Dog, black and white, good, clear transfer, 2³/₈″. Price range: $50.00 to 65.00.

Mugs #3 Deer Stalking, hunters and dogs, brown transfer, 2⁵/₈″. Price range: $45.00 to 58.00; To Washington The Deliverer, eagle, rose on white, 2³/₈″, very early and very rare. Price range: $350.00 to 475.00; Cricket, game, boy batting, colored transfer, 2⁵/₈″. Price range: $45.00 to 58.00.

Mugs #4 Two Hunters, on horses, palm tree, 2³/₄″. Price range; $45.00 to 55.00; Attention, girl, cats and an adult, 2³/₄″. Price range: $50.00 to 58.00; The Butterfly, two girls after butterflies, cats on a fence, girl with a basket, 2¹/₂″. Price range: $50.00 to 58.00; Flowers of Literature, man with tray on head, 2⁵/₈″. Price range: $50.00 to 58.00.

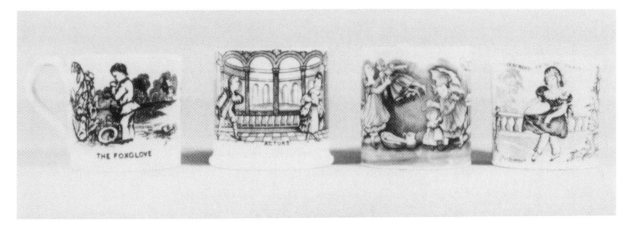

Mugs #5 The Foxglove, black on white, boy with plant, 2⁵/₈″, one of a series having to do with plants. Price range: $58.00 to 68.00; Actors, aqua transfer, girl and boy on stage, 2⁷/₈″. Price range: $48.00 to 58.00; Children with Umbrellas and Dolls, colored transfers, 2³/₄″. Price range: $50.00 to 68.00; Teaching Tray To Dance, girl holding skirts, dancing, rose on white, 2¹/₂″. Price range: $58.00 to 68.00.

13

Mugs #6 Peg In The Ring, girls in a game, transfers of yellow, red, green, red ring around inside lip, 2³/₄″. Price range: $60.00 to 70.00; The Swing, black on white, children with bow and arrows, girls in swing, 2³/₄″. Price range: $45.00 to 50.00; Northern Spell, transfers of black, white, yellow, green, red, red lip around rim, children playing, 2³/₄″. Price range: $58.00 to 68.00; Blind Man's Bluff, 2³/₄″. Price range: $58.00 to 68.00; He Thast By The Plough Would Thrive, Himself Must Either Hold Or Drive, 2³/₄″. Price range: $55.00 to 60.00.

Mugs #7 Boy And Pie, girl and boy in a garden, 2½″. Price range: $58.00 to 68.00; Girl and Soldier, red, yellow and black, 2½″. Price range: $70.00 to 90.00; Two Soldiers, 2¾″. Price range: $70.00 to 90.00; Boys In A Fight, four boys, two in a fight, brown, green. Price range: $58.00 to 68.00; Pig Feeding, pigs, house, fence, 2¾″. Price range: $65.00 to 75.00.

Mugs #8 Prosper Freedom, mulberry on white, 2½″, eagle on reverse side, rare. Price range: $200.00 to 225.00; Girl and Soldier, green transfer, girl has apron. Price range: $65.00 to 85.00; Two Hunters, mulberry colored transfer, 3″, Edge Malkin & Co. Price range: $65.00 to 85.00; Single Hunter, 2½″. Price range: $70.00 to 90.00.

Mugs #9 Emma, name in a mulberry-flowered wreath, 2½". Price range: $95.00 to 110.00; A Gift For Hannah, luster rim, 2⅜". Price range: $100.00 to 125.00; Henry, black on white, leaves, 2½". Price range: $85.00 to 100.00; Maria, black on white, flowered borders at the top and bottom. Price range: $125.00 to 150.00.

Mugs #10 Eliza, light blue on white, 2⅝". Price range: $85.00 to 100.00; Dorothy, rim of flowers, 2⅝". Price range: $85.00 to 100.00; Susan, black on white, 2⅛", with alphabet rim embossed. Price range: $125.00 to 150.00; Frederick, blue name in wreath, 2½". Price range: $85.00 to 100.00.

Mugs #11 A Mother's Affection, girl in a swing on back of mug, blue on white, 2⅝". Price range: $75.00 to 90.00; The Seasons, August, black on white, people working in garden, one of a monthly series. Price range: $100.00 to 125.00; History of the House That Jack Built, green transfer, 2⅜". Price range: $85.00 to 95.00; From Thee The World Expects, brown on white, may have something to do with the British postal system, 2⅜". Price range: $65.00 to 75.00.

Mugs #12 God Bless The Land We Live In, orange and rust on white, 2½″. Price range: $150.00 to 175.00; Reward of Merit, this saying enclosed in a wreath, 2½″. Price range: $95.00 to 125.00; A Present For My Dear Boy, blue on grayish body, 2⅜″. Price range: $85.00 to 100.00; For Loving A Book, redish-orange on white, 2″. Price range: $75.00 to 95.00.

Mugs #13 *Canary (colored), see also color picture in appropriate section, top row left to right, first and fifth mugs are the same, poppy, 2¼″. Price range: $175.00 to 225.00; A Trifle For Margaret, 2¼″. Price range: $225.00 to 250.00; A Present For A Good Girl, black pictures of girl with a cross, 2¼″. Price range: $200.00 to 225.00; For My Favorite Girl, 2¼″. Price range: $175.00 to 225.00; Row Two, left to right--Draping Ropes of Luster, blue, green, red, leaf (type) design, 2¼″. Price range: $175.00 to 225.00; A Newfoundland Dog For Robert, red transfer, 2⅜″. Price range: $250.00 to 275.00; Lafayette-Washington, two mugs in this picture are the same except one is a red transfer and the other black, very rare, Leed's type. Price range: black, $700.00 to 800.00, red, $800.00 to 1,000.00; Lady With Basket and Dog, weeping willow tree, 2¼″. Price range: $150.00 to 200.00.

Note: Canary earthernware dates to the early 1800's and was produced by English potters in the Staffordshire district. The body of this product is yellow in color and is usually decorated with transfer printing. There are early examples of hand painted products as well.

Mugs #14 Lady Feeding Hens. Price range: $55.00 to 68.00; The Judge, black transfer, 2⅝″. Price range: $40.00 to 45.00; Franklin Maxim: Little Strokes Fell Great Oaks, wood chopper, 2½″. Price range: $100.00 to 150.00; "A" Was An Apple That Grew On A Tree, "B" with a boat, inside writing on rim, "C" 2⅝″. Price range: $75.00 to 95.00.

Mugs #15 Nursery Rhyme Egg Cup, Old Mother Hubbard. Price range: $10.00 to 12.00; (2) Staffordshire cups and saucers from a child's tea set, cups, 2″ tall, saucers, 4¾″. Price range: $20.00 to 22.00 each; Merry Christmas, cup and saucer to a child's tea set. Price range: $30.00 to 35.00 each cup and saucer; Bottom row--Cheap Shop, mug with people shopping, Buy What Thou Hast No Need Of and Ere Long Thou Wilt Sell Thy Necessaries, 2½″. Price range: $100.00 to 150.00; Dr. Franklin's Poor Richard: Miners Handle Your Tools Without Mittens--Remember The Cat In Gloves Catches More Mice, 2⅛″. Price range: $100.00 to 150.00; Sloth Like Rust Consumes, boy by water, boy in water, boy with key, 2¾″. Price range: $100.00 to 150.00; Debts, person at door, seated person and a woman. Price range: $100.00 to 150.00; Franklin Maxim, No Gains Without Pains, 2¹/₈″. Price range: $100.00 to 150.00.

17

Mugs #16 "V" "W" "X", boy whipping another, rose transfer, 2⅞". Price range: $75.00 to 85.00; Feeding The Chickens, mulberry transfer, pink luster, 2½". Price range: $95.00 to 110.00; Horse, mulberry (colored) transfer of a horse, 2¼", may be from an animal series. Price range: $65.00 to 75.00; A Slothful Boy Fortells An Idle Man, 2⅜", pink. Price range: $95.00 to 120.00.

Mugs #17 "K" Is For Kitten That Plays With A Ball, cat picture with kite, 2⅝". Price range: $100.00 to 125.00; "N" and "O" letters in red with owl, red lip ring, 2¾". Price range: $100.00 to 125.00; "P" Parrot, 2⅝". Price range: $100.00 to 125.00; "T" lady in blue and boy in red, red lip ring, 2½". Price range: $100.00 to 125.00; "X" red, lady hearing a child read, "W" Christ with cross, 2¾". Price range: $100.00 to 125.00.

Mugs #18 Fishing Party, colored transfer of two children, 2¾". Price range: $65.00 to 75.00; Children Shooting Bow, other side is child and dog, black and white, 2⅝". Price range: $65.00 to 75.00; The Boar Hunt, colored transfer, 2½". Price range: $75.00 to 85.00; "H" Begins Horse Whose Paces Are Swift, "G" Stand For Gander, 2⅝". Price range: $100.00 to 125.00.

Mugs #19 "B" Is For Ball As Round As Can Be, "A" Stands for Apple which Here You May See, nice transfers, 2⅝". Price range: $100.00 to 125.00; "D" is For Dash Who nicely Sits Up, "C" Begins Cat, 2⅞". Price range: $100.00 to 125.00; "M" "N" "O" Whip-Top, children with whips, 3". Price range: $100.00 to 125.00; "F" Begins Fox And We Know He Is Sly, "E" is For Elephant Monstrous and High; beige colored mug with red rim, 2¾". Price range: $100.00 to 125.00; "H" with picture of horse, "G" with a gander and foliage, 2⅝". Price range: $100.00 to 125.00.

Mugs #20 Top row, left to right–Stripes, green with gold luster, red with gold luster, cobalt with gold luster, red ring around its base, 2⅜". Price range: $75.00 to 78.00; Complete Alphabet, gray mug with cobalt trim, yellow dots separating A B C's, 2¼", may be Leeds. Price range: $125.00 to 150.00; Sponge (type), ware in blue on white, 1⅞". Price range: $100.00 to 125.00; Pink Luster Floral, orange flowers, shell type design between flowers, 2⅝". Price range: $100.00 to 150.00; Person With Head Burden, flow blue on white. Price range: $100.00 to 150.00; Wagon Wheel, cobalt flowing blue with luster, 2¾", see complete tea set in this book. Price range: $100.00 to 125.00; Flow Blue Criss-Crossing of green, rust, gold, 2⅝". Price range: $100.00 to 125.00.

Mugs #21 Top row, left to right: Spiral Shell, luster. Price range: $90.00 to 125.00; Blue Bells; flowers with green, fan leaves between blue flowers. Price range: $90.00 to 125.00; Floral Overlap; design goes inside mug, red, blue, green, 2¾″. Price range: $75.00 to 85.00; Fan, cobalt fan flower with gold luster, rust and green, 2⅛″. Price range: $75.00 to 100.00; Lustered Bird, 1⅞″. Price range: $75.00 to 100.00.

Lunch Boxes Tin Lunch Box, same type on either side of second row, Peter Rabbit On Parade, 4⅛″ long, condition is most important factor in pricing these boxes. Price range: $65.00 to 75.00.

Tin Mugs Rattle Mugs, very rare, must be in good codition even though rare, 3″ shepherd; the other is a tin with flowers and ducks, rattles are hidden but heard. Price range: $150.00 to 225.00 each.

Mugs #22 Bird, black transfer of bird on grayish mug with blue, 2⅜″. Price range: $55.00 to 65.00; Alphabet, divided by flowered strip, brown underglaze print with birds and branches as decorative design, 2⅞″ crested wren, matching plate shown in plate section. Price range: $45.00 to 55.00; Fox and Goose, rose transfer, 2⅞″. Price range: $45.00 to 60.00; Alphabet, divided by flower strip, same as second one in #22. Price range: $45.00 to 55.00.

Mugs #23 German Whistle Mug, not as old as previous mugs, 1900's, two children fishing, handle has a bird whistle, collection--Hamilton. Price range: $38.00 to 40.00.

Mugs #24 Frances Alden, boy drinking from a bowl. Price range: $20.00 to 22.00.

Mugs #25 Kate Greenaway (style) hand painted mug, 3″ x 3½″. Price range: $20.00 to 22.00; Alice In Wonderland, Mad Hatter's Tea Party, 3″ x 3″, collection--Schmoker. Price range: $20.00 to 22.00.

Children's China Plates

Plates particularly for children were produced by many of the potters of the past. Many were executed with cheap decorations and less than perfect enamelling. The borders of the plates frequently carried a moulded daisy or alphabet design. Commemorative transfers appeared on several as did Franklin Maxims.

Franklin's pithy maxims carried warnings and instructions about thrift and hard work. There was usually a picture with one of the following titles: Dr. Franklin's Maxims, Poor Richard's Maxims or Franklin's Maxims. These plates date around 1875 with Buckley Wood and Company or Bates, Walker & Company as likely candidates for the title of producer.

If more than one plate is shown in a picture, the description will start with the top row and move left to right.

China Plates #1 A B C D Bird, matches a mug in Mugs #22, collection--Hamilton. Price range: $45.00 to 55.00.

China Plates #2 He That By The Plough Would Thrive, colored leaf border, Franklin mottoes, 4¾", collection--private. Price range: $95.00 to 110.00; Oriental, chinoiserie, colored transfers, animal and butterfly, dog border, 6⅛", collection--private. Price range: $55.00 to 65.00; Benevolence Is Commendable In All Persons, colorful flower rim, three persons, 4³/₄", collection--private. Price range: $95.00 to 110.00; Farming Plates, both with embossed alphabet borders and country scenes, first plate has house, horses, cart and man, second plate has a man plowing under a tree, embossed alphabet on both, collection--private. Price range: $75.00 to 95.00.

China Plates #3 The Mischievous Cat, embossed flower border, green transfer, Davenport (word) and anchor on base, 7¼″, 8-sided, collection--private. Price range: $85.00 to 95.00; Old Mother Hubbard, embossed rim, 7⅜″, collection--private. Price range: $75.00-85.00; Frolics of Youth, The Young Artist, alphabet rim, 7¼″, Frolics of Youth, The Fall of China, 7¼″, series plates, collection--private. Price range: $75.00 to 100.00; The Village Blacksmith, beige plate, alphabet rim, colored, collection--private. Price range: $65.00 to 75.00.

China Plates #4 Soldiers, first and last plates on top row, blue edge ring, 5⅞″, collection--private. Price range: $65.00 to 75.00; Docteur (sic) Doctor, 6⅜″, collection--private. Price range: $75.00 to 85.00; Two People, embossed, early, rare, collection--private. Price range: $100.00 to 125.00; Child and Bird, bat printing, impressed "B", rust, colored figure, 4½″, collection--private. Price range: $100.00 to 125.00.

China Plates #5 Sacred History of Joseph and his Brethren, series of 7½″ plates with vivid decals and a daisy (raised) border, Joseph's first dream, Joseph making himself known to his brethren, Potiphar's wife falsely accusing Joseph, Joseph interpreting the dreams of Pharaoh's chief butler and baker, Judah resigning himself and brethren into the hands of Joseph, Joseph's brethern applying to him for corn in time of famine, all "s's" are printed as "f's", early series, collection--private. Price range: $325.00 to 375.00 (set).

China Plates #6 Now I Have A Cow, bead and alphabet border, 5⅛″, Franklin Maxim, collection--private. Price range: $95.00 to 110.00; Three Children and a Train, 7″, flowered rim, center is mulberry colored transfer, collection--private. Price range: $95.00 to 110.00; Experience Keeps A Dear School, beaded alphabet border, 5⅛″, transfers, collection--private. Price range $100.00 to 125.00; Tiger, Kangaroo, first and last plates on bottom row, 8-sided polychrome borders with rope-like edges, sepia transfer of tiger and kanguroo (sic), collection--private. Price range: $75.00 to 95.00; On The River Bank, children fishing, flowered border, 5⅝″, collection--private. Price range: $75.00 to 90.00.

Royal Doulton Cups, Saucers, Tumblers, Plates and Bowls

Royal Doulton #1 Nursery Tales variety, cream-colored, some crazing, cup and tumbler numbered 764873. Footed tumbler, 3¾"; mug, 2¾"; small plate, 6¼"; large plate, 7¼", collection--Schmoker. Price range: tumbler, $45.00 to 65.00; mug, $35.00 to 45.00; plates, $35.00 to 48.00 each; cup and saucer, $45.00 to 68.00.

Royal Doulton #2 Where Are You Going My Pretty Maid, copyright Nursery Rhymes. Plates, left to right: 6", 9", 7", collection--Schmoker. Price range: $35.00 to 58.00 each.

Royal Doulton #3 Old Mother Goose, all but the tumbler contain the verse. Tumbler, 3¾"; plates: 7", 8", collection--Schmoker. Price range: plates, $35.00 to 48.00 each, cup and saucer, $45.00 to 68.00, tumbler, $45.00 to 65.00.

Royal Doulton #4 Ride A Cock Horse, one of the copyright Royal Doulton series members, entire verse appears on the plate and on the back of the pitcher. Plate, 7"; pitcher, 4¼", collection--Schmoker. Price range: plate, $35.00 to 48.00; pitcher, $48.00 to 58.00

Royal Doulton #5 Little Miss Muffet, porcelain, Doulton mark, no verse, just the line to identify Little Miss Muffet, collection--Schmoker. Price range: $48.00 to 68.00.

Royal Doulton #6 Hey Diddle Diddle, copyright Nursery Rhymes. Plate, 8"; tumbler, 3¾", collection--Schmoker. Price range: cup and saucer, $45.00 to 68.00; tumbler, $45.00 to 65.00; plate, $35.00 to 48.00.

Royal Doulton #7 Old Mother Hubbard, copyright Nursery Rhymes. Cup, 3½" diameter and 2½" tall; saucer, 5½", collection--Schmoker. Price range: $45.00 to 68.00.

Royal Doulton #8 Little Bo Peep, left to right: 8", 6" plates, collection--Schmoker. Price range: $35.00 to 48.00.

Royal Doulton #9 There Was A Little Man and He Had A Little Gun, copyright Nursery Rhymes. Mug, 2¾"; plate, 7"; bowl 5½" diameter, collection--Schmoker. Price range: mug, $35.00 to 45.00; plate, $35.00 to 48.00; cup and saucer, $45.00 to 68.00; bowl, $48.00 to 58.00.

Royal Doulton #10 The Queen of Hearts, pastel colors; To Market, To Market; Mary, Mary Quite Contrary, pastel colors, collection--Schmoker. Price range: plates, $35.00 to 48.00.

Royal Doulton #11 Little Tom Tucker, copyright Nursery Rhymes. Plates, 8", 9"; saucer, 5½", collection--Schmoker. Price range: $35.00 to 48.00.

Note: Established in Lambeth in 1815 by John Doulton and John Watts, the firm was known as Doulton & Company after Mr. Watts retired in 1854. In 1901, King Edward VII presented the Royal Warrant allowing the company to use the word "royal" in the product description. Much of this company's ware came to America. The company is still in business.

Miscellaneous Beverage Sets in China
Miniature Beverage Sets

Beverage Set #1 Greenaway Basket and Jugs, set consists of two jugs, a basket and six tiny (punch-bowl-size) cups, France, marked "Sarreguemine", cream-colored body, burgandy line trim, decals of children, animals and sports equipment on all pieces, jug, 5¼" tall; cup, 1½" tall; basket, 9" long, 5" wide, 7½" high including the handle, collection--Lechler. Price range: $225.00 to 275.00.

Beverage Set #2 Beer Set, eight pieces, brown and green on cream, Germany, possibly Charlottenbrunn, Silesia, Germany, Josef Schachtel, circa 1859-1919, possibly electrotechnical porcelain. Tray, 4" with indented circles for small 1¼" steins; main stein, 2½" tall, collection--Lechler. Price range: $145.00 to 175.00.

Beverage Set #3 Bavaria Stein Set, stein, 1⅞"; tray 5¾" x 7⅞" marked Mitterteich, colorful children, collection--Lechler. Price range $20.00 to 30.00.

28

Tea Sets and Dinner Sets

* indicates items shown in the color section.

ENGLISH TEA SETS, FLOWERS, BANDS AND FANCY TRIMS

Creamware

Known Pattern Pieces: This picture contains more than one partial set.

Point of Origin, Date: England; second half of the 18th century

Colors, Ware Type, Features: Refined cream-colored earthenware; some crazing

Measurements: Accurate measurements are unavailable; these are child-size rather than doll house size

Classification: Very rare

Collection: Strong Museum card catalogue references, 77, 3617, 77, 3616

Price Range for Complete Sets in Good Condition: Complete sets are rarely found

References or Author's Comments: Cream-colored ware was introduced around 1760 to replace early salt-glazed stoneware and delft (type) earthenwares. Most English potteries produced this type of ware from 1770.

Leed's Floral

Known Pattern Pieces: Tea set

Point of Origin, Date: England; Leeds Pottery, Jacl Lane, Hunslett, Leeds Yorkshire; circa early 1800's

Colors, Ware Type, Features: Underglaze flowers in blue, slightly flown; grayish body

Measurements: Teapot, 3¾"; sugar, 3½"

Classification: Very rare

Collection: Lechler

Price Range for Complete Sets in Good Condition: $425.00 to 525.00

References or Author's Comments: Leeds Pottery, 1758-1820, sometimes called Leeds Old Pottery; Hartley, Greens & Co. operated it from 1771. It was known for overglaze transfer-printing in red and black on creamware from 1775 to around 1790. Pearlware became popular then and at the turn of the century, underglaze printing in blue took over. Refer to *The Dictionary of Blue and White Printed Pottery 1780-1880* by Coysh and Henrywood for further details on Leed's ware.

Cherry Tree

Known Pattern Pieces: Tea Set

Point of Origin, Date: England; circa 1830

Colors, Ware Type, Features: Hand painted cherry design on earthenware; handleless cups

Measurements: Teapot, 5"; sugar, 4½"; creamer, 3½"; cup (no handle), about 2"; plate, 4½"

Classification: Rare

Collection: Lechler

Price Range for Complete Sets in Good Condition: $250.00 to 375.00

*LONDON SHAPE WITH BLUE BLOSSOMS

Known Pattern Pieces: Tea sets with waste bowls
Point of Origin, Date: England; Rogers, Dale Hall, Longport, Staffordshire Potteries; circa 1815-1836
Colors, Ware Type, Features: Underglaze hand painted blue flowers on London-shape earthenware; good quality; five different cup sizes and shapes with the London type teapot; also, two wastebowl sizes and shapes with the London style teapot
Identical Blanks with Different Decorations: Brown and pink enamel on white; Broseley pattern (a chinoiserie design with a willow tree, two men on a bridge, and a pagoda-type temple in mirror image); Adam Buck style prints, black and buff and black on white with pink luster trim; sepia and buff; black printed flowers; pink luster scenic decoration
Measurements: Teapot, 3⅞"; sugar, 3"; creamer, 2"; cups, 1 ¹⁵/₁₆", 1½", 1¾"; saucer 4¼"; waste bowl, 2½" tall and 3½" across
Classification: Rare
Collection: Lechler
Price Range for Complete Sets in Good Condition: $375.00 to 500.00
References or Author's Comments: Several differently decorated sets are found in Milbourn's book. The set shown here is also shown in *Antiques In Miniature* by McClinton with the waste bowl and the name "Rogers" impressed in the ware. The painted sets are the earliest ones, followed by the blue on white, black on buff and the over glaze sepia print on buff.

The three teapots in this group shot are representative teapots showing different available designs in toy ware:
Left to right: Blue Blossoms; Ma Mammy Dance A Baby; Josephine and L'Aiglon

Adam Buck (style) Prints

Known Pattern Pieces: Teapot, water or coffee pot, creamers, sugar, waste bowl, egg cups, cups and saucers
Point of Origin, Date: England; circa 1820-1825
Colors, Ware Type, Features: Cream-colored ware with Adam Buck (style) of bat printing on the London (shaped) teapot; woman and child
Identical Blanks with Different Decorations: London (shaped) teapot and matching pieces have several different types of decorations appearing on the set of blanks
Measurements: Teapot, 3 ⁷/₁₆", sugar, 3"; creamer, 2"; cups: 1½", 1¹⁵/₁₆"; saucer, 4¼"; waste bowl, 2½" tall and 3½" across; coffee pot, 5½"
Classification: Very rare
Collection: Steffen
Price Range for Complete Sets in Good Condition: $500.00 to 1,000.00
References or Author's Comments: Milbourn states that there are two shapes and sizes in the waste bowls and sugar bowls.

Rogers' Blue and White

Known Pattern Pieces: Tea set
Point of Origin, Date: England; Rogers, Dale Hall, Longport, Staffordshire Potteries, Earthenware; circa 1815-1842
Colors, Ware Type, Features: Blue on white birds, flowers and butterflies; very deep saucers; quality ware; decorative giant indented spaces--two to a side on the three main pieces of this set

Measurements: Teapot, 3½″; sugar, 3½″; creamer, 2¼″; cup, 1¾″; saucer, 4½″

Classification: Rare

Collection: Lechler

Price Range for Complete Sets in Good Condition: $375.00 to 425.00

References or Author's Comments: "Rogers" impressed on this ware.

Wind Flower

Known Pattern Pieces: Tea set with waste bowl and two plates

Point of Origin, Date: England; circa 1825-1835

Colors, Ware Type, Features: Flow blue decoration on thin earthenware; Anemone type (field flowers) with dark petals and white centers; thin, flat, deeply set lids on covered pieces; anemone is a small plant--one variety is known as Wind Flower

Identical Blanks with Different Decorations: Peafowl, see Milbourn book, pages 43 and 44

Measurements: Teapot, 2⅝″; sugar, 2⅝″; creamer, 2″; cup, 1½″; saucer, 4½″; plate, 4¼″; waste bowl, 2″ tall and 3½″ across

Classification: Very rare in either Peafowl or Flow Blue

Collection: Lechler

Price Range for Complete Sets in Good Condition: $800.00 to 1,200.00

References or Author's Comments: This is an example of an early set having a waste bowl. In Milbourn's book it is said that this set might have been thrown rather than moulded. This author does not agree.

*Meigh's Moss Rose (correct name); Green Clover; People and Steeple

Known Pattern Pieces: Three tea sets on this blank; known dinner set in Moss Rose

Point of Origin, Date: England; C.M. & S., Charles Meigh & Son (marked); Hanley, Staffordshire Potteries; Old Hall Pottery; circa 1851-61; People and Steeple, circa 1835-49

Colors, Ware Type, Features: Moss Rose is blue on white; Clover is green on white; People and Steeple is light blue on white; earthenware; tilt-blossom finials

Identical Blanks with Different Decorations: Moss Rose; Green Clover; People and Steeple

Measurements: Teapot 4″; sugar, 3¾″; creamer, 2″; cup, 2″; saucer, 4½″; plate, 5″; waste bowl, 2¾″ tall and 4½″ across rim; cups without handles, 1¾″ tall

Classification: Rare

Collection: Lechler

Price Range for Complete Sets in Good Condition: $375.00 to 450.00

References or Author's Comments: For C.M. & S. Moss Rose marking see Godden, page 429; of the three sets, People and Steeple is the earliest because of the light blue color and the cups without handles.

*Dimmocks Blue Band

Known Pattern Pieces: Tea set with waste bowl

Point of Origin, Date: England; Thomas Dimmock (Junr) & Co., Staffordshire Potteries; 1828-59

Colors, Ware Type, Features: Blue (which flows now and then) on white; interesting cup handles; marked with intertwined double D

Identical Blanks with Different Decorations: In Milbourn's book on page 60, there is a set with underglaze green print (sheet) pattern showing stars and dots. The matching dinner set may be seen on page 116 in the same book

Measurements: Teapot, 4¼″; sugar, 3½″; creamer, 2½″; cup, 2″; saucer, 4½; plate, 6″; waste bowl, 2½″ tall and 4¼″ across

Classification: Rare

Collection: Lechler

Price Range for Complete Sets in Good Condition: $225.00 to 350.00

References or Author's Comments: To see impressed monogram, look on page 208 in Godden's *Encyclopedia of British Pottery and Porcelain Marks*

Godwin No. 26

Known Pattern Pieces: Tea set

Point of Origin, Date: England, Sneyd Green, Cobridge; J.R. Godwin (John and Robert Godwin); circa 1834-1866; Peacock set marked "B.G." for Benjamine E. Godwin, 1834-41

Colors, Ware Type, Features: Blue, yellow, brown, and green floral design on white earthenware; main pieces are footed

Identical Blanks with Different Decorations: Peacock (marked "B.G."); also a bird set in Flow Blue

Measurements: Teapot, 4¼″; sugar, 3¾″; creamer, 2½″; cup, 1¾″; saucer, 4½″; plate, 5″; waste bowl, 2½″ tall and 4⅓″ across

Classification: Obtainable

Collection: Lechler

Price Range for Complete Sets in Good Condition: $300.00 to 375.00

References or Author's Comments: The set in Flow Blue would be more expensive. Godden noted on page 277 of *Encyclopedia of British Pottery and Porcelain Marks,* that Benjamin E. Godwin produced many child's toy services with the "B.G." mark

Canary soft paste mugs: Poppy (first and last on top row); A Trifle For Margaret; A Present For A Good Girl; For My Favorite Girl. Bottom Row, left to right: Draping Ropes of Luster; A Newfoundland Dog For Robert; (2) Lafayette-Washington (rare); Lady With Basket And Dog. Private Collection.

London (Shape) with Blue Flowers tea ware, England, Rogers, circa 1815-1836, handpainted. Lechler Collection.

Meigh's Moss Rose (Moss Rose is correct name), England, C.M. & S., Charles Meigh and Son, circa 1851-1861. Lechler Collection.

33

Dimmock's Blue Band tea set, England, circa 1828-1859, Thomas Dimmock (Junr) & Co. Lechler Collection.

Columbia Star (correct name) tea set, England, 1840, designed for the William Henry Harrison campaign of 1840, rare. Lechler Collection.

Amherst Japan tea equipage, England, rare. Lechler Collection.

Woman By The Urn tea ware, England, circa 1850-1860. Lechler Collection.

Birds and Holly tea set for six, England, hand-painted. Lechler Collection.

Ferns and Flowers dinner set, England, circa 1822-1825, adult ware and toy ware attributed to Charles Keeling (applied C.K. impressed on a raised pad). Lechler Collection.

Tower dinner set, England, Copeland and Garrett, circa 1820-1830, Spode Works, Stoke, Staffordshire. Lechler Collection.

Hackwood's Blue Willow dinner set, England, circa 1827-1843, "Hackwood" impressed on bases. Lechler Collection.

Monastery Hill or Institution dinner ware, England, circa 1827-1843, Hackwood. Lechler Collection.

Garden Sports dinner set, England, circa 1842.
Lechler Collection.

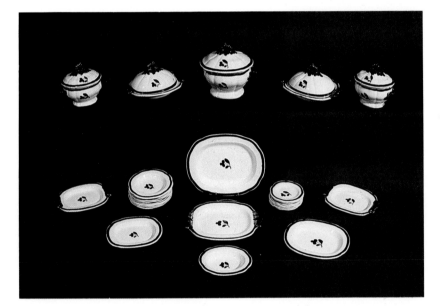

Copper Luster Tea Leaf (Variant) dinner set,
England, circa 1835-1849. Fredrick Collection.

Asiatic Birds (Flow Blue) dinner set, England,
Charles Meigh, circa 1835-1849. Lechler Collection.

Forget-Me-Not (Flow Blue) dinner set, England, Private Collection.

Seaweed With Arrows dinner set, England, circa 1851-1861, Charles Meigh & Son, Old Hall Pottery, Hanley, Staffordshire. Lechler Collection.

Chinese Red and Cobalt dinner set, England. Lechler Collection.

Pearl dessert set, England, circa 1867-1889, marked "Pearl" with a beehive. Lechler Collection.

Rhodesia (correct name) dinner set, Ridgway, circa 1900-1915, same set of blanks as Humphrey's Clock. Lechler Collection.

Christmas tea set, Germany, circa 1890-1900. Private Collection.

Steiff animals and clowns with German Circus tea or coffee set. Hartzfeld Collection.

French Packaging tea set with no creamer or sugar in the original package, this set never taken from the basket. Lechler Collection.

Paris Scenic, France, circa 1890-1910, hand-painted. Lechler Collection.

French Children's housekeeping set, marked "Luneville K.G. France," large dinner set with unusual pieces. Lechler Collection.

Steiff rabbit and bear with Sports Minded Bears tea set. Hartzfeld Collection.

Steiff rabbit with Scenic Pink Luster tea or coffee set from Czechosolvakia. Hartzfeld Collection.

Toy enamel ware for the kitchen. Lechler Collection.

Invitation to Tea from a straw stuffed, fully jointed bear; European Speckled (Enamel Ware) tea set; Writing box with chamberstick, wax and sealer. Knight and Lechler Collections.

Cherries on Enameled Ware, tea for six, European, circa 1890-1920, also available with floral designs (see Kitchen #7 in text). Lechler Collection. Straw stuffed, fully jointed bear, 18″ tall, shoe button eyes, black thread nose and feet. Knight Collection.

Early Steiff Bear, fully jointed and straw stuffed; child's picnic basket with a Pabst beer bottle sample, 4½″ tall. Knight and Lechler Collections.

German enamel ware tea set; tablecloth made from handkerchiefs by Elizabeth Hall Anderson. Lechler Collection.

German enamel ware in the original box from the Bing Toy Company. Lechler Collection.

Bear on a Picnic, fully jointed, hump on back and straw stuffed; child's picnic basket; red ware bowl; blue enamel creamer from a complete tea set; sapphire tumble up. Knight and Lechler Collections.

43

Enameled sand toys and bear: sand toys, circa 1914; bear, fully jointed, leather paws and feet, embroidered nose and mouth, 18″ tall. Knight Collection.

Early Red Ware miniature churn from the Hamilton Collection; early glass miniature rolling pin from the Lechler Collection.

Cherry corner cupboard, 53½″ at highest point. Lechler Collection.

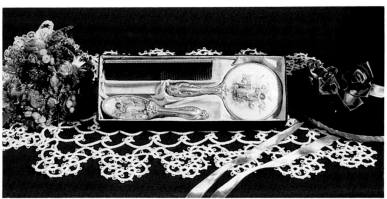

Grooming set with painting on porcelain, in the original box. Lechler Collection.

Playhouse dressing room with corner what-not-stand in walnut; Larkin (style) cupboard for dresses or books with a drop-front desk, see Bedroom #8 in text; Desk, 34″ tall. Lechler Collection.

Chamber and dresser sets in miniature. Lechler Collection.

French wash stand with china accessories marked "K. & G. Luneville France." Lechler Collection.

Tumble ups in miniature. Lechler Collection.

Tumble ups: Sapphire With Handle, 4″ tall; Cobalt Swirl, 5″ tall; Nailsea, 3¼″ tall; Plate, 3¾″ across; Blue Etched With Handle, 5″; Flare-Bottomed, 4½″. Lechler Collection.

Dutch boudoir (green glass) chamber set; Nursery Rhyme punch cup with a matching lid serves as a potty. Welker Collection.

Decorative ewers and basins from the mid-nineteenth century. Smith Collection.

Chamber sets, probably Boston & Sandwich Glass Company, Sandwich, MA, circa 1835-1850. Corning Glass Museum Collection.

Covered tureens, probably Boston and Sandwich Glass Company, Sandwich, MA, circa 1835-1850. Corning Glass Museum Collection.

Top left: Bees, Bears and Honey: large brown bear, 19″ tall, straw stuffed, shoe button eyes; small Steiff, 12″ bear with unmarked button in his ear, collection and photo: Gene Austin; *Top right:* Gold Bears: straw stuffed 13″ and 14″ bears, fully jointed, one with shoe button eyes, one with glass eyes; front bear has four embroidered toes on each foot, collection and picture: Gene Austin; *Bottom left:* Christmas Bears: bear on left is a 19″ straw stuffed, fully jointed bear with shoe button eyes and embroidered nose; 9″ bear has glass eyes and a squeeker, fully jointed, embroidered nose, collection and picture: Gene Austin; *Bottom right:* Ready To Go! Front bear is a 12″ Steiff, straw stuffed and fully jointed, rust embroidered nose; middle bear is 12½″ long, dark brown embroidered nose and mouth; back bear is a 13″ Steiff, straw stuffed, glass eyes, embroiderd toes and paws collection and picture: Gene Austin.

47

Top left: Bears on a Quilt: back bear is 25″ tall, straw stuffed, shoe button eyes; front bears are both Steiff, shoe button eyes on one, glass eyes on the other, straw stuffed; handmade quilt shows the story of the "Three Little Pigs", collection and picture: Gene Austin; *Top right:* Margaret Woodbury Strong Bears; three new bears from the Strong Museum in Rochester, New York, collection and picture: Gene Austin; *Bottom left:* Bears At School: 18″ glass eyed bear, fully jointed, straw stuffed, embroidered (four toes) and paws; 12″ Steiff brown bear with shoe button eyes, straw stuffed; old slate hide bound, collection and picture: Gene Austin; *Bottom right:* Steiff: back bear, 13″ tall, glass eyes, straw stuffed, hump on back; front bear is 12″ tall, straw stuffed, shoe button eyes, long curving arms, embroidered nose, collection and picture: Gene Austin.

48

Davenport's Pink Luster Blossoms

Known Pattern Pieces: Tea sets in two different blank styles
Point of Origin, Date England; Davenport; 1836; "Davenport" in an arc over an anchor, with a "3" on one side and a six on the other side
Colors, Ware Type, Features: Superb example of Davenport in an unusual bunch-melon shape with pink and copper luster; lusty blossoms trimmed with green and mauve; the cup handles match those on the teapot and creamer; 701 hand painted on each
Identical Blanks with Different Decorations: The same decorations are on a later set shown in Milbourn's book on pages 56 and 57
Measurements: Teapot, 2¾" tall; sugar, 2¾" tall; creamer, 1¾"; cup, 1¾" tall; saucer, 4¼"; waste bowl, 2¼" tall and 4¼" across
Classification: Very rare
Collection: Lechler
Price Range for Complete Sets in Good Condition: $500.00 to 600.00
References or Author's Comments: See Godden's page 189 for correct Davenport mark and Milbourn's book for different blank style, but with the same decorations. (This author has seen two blanks mixed in one set, but believe this to be a put-together.) Luster decoration was developed by John Hancock of Hanley, England, in the early 1800's. The copper, bronze, ruby, gold, purple, yellow, pink and mottled pink luster finishes were created from gold. This decoration was painted on the glazed object and fired. Pink luster is referred to as "Sunderland Luster". The pink tones vary in color and pattern.

*COLUMBIA STAR (correct name)

Known Pattern Pieces: Tea set
Point of Origin, Date England; 1840; Jno, Ridgway
Colors, Ware Type, Features: Light blue on white earthenware; also known in green, brown, black, pink; large stars surrounded by smaller stars with a log cabin; log cabin seen in bottom of each handleless cup
Measurements: Teapot, 4¼"; sugar, 4"; creamer, 2¾"; cup, 1¾"; saucer, 4". (A second style teapot is shown. It is in mulberry and is from the Kuran collection.)
Classification: Very rare
Collection: Lechler
Price Range for Complete Sets in Good Condition: $1,500.00 to 2,000.00
References or Author's Comments: The Columbia Star or Log Cabin design was created for the William Henry Harrison campaign of 1840. In a double elipse the following mark is found on toy ware: "Columbia Star Oct. 28th 1840 Jno, Ridgway"

Sprig

Known Pattern Pieces Tea set; dinner set
Point of Origin, Date England; circa 1840
Colors, Ware Type, Features: Thick body; delicate and sparse hand painted flowers in various colors
Identical Blanks with Different Decorations: Sprig designs were very popular, so they came in various colors on many different blanks
Measurements: Teapot, 4¼″; sugar, 4¼″; creamer, 2¾″; cup without handles, 2½″ tall and 2½″ across (cups will vary in size and design); saucer, 4¼″. Dinner set; long, covered tureen, 5″ x 5½″; platter, 5½″ long; open server, 1½″ tall (2); covered tureen, 3½″; soup, 4½″; plates, 3¼″, 3½″
Classification: Rare
Collection: Lechler
Price Range for Complete Sets in Good Condition: Tea set, $325.00 to 400.00; dinner set $350.00 to 425.00

Colors, Ware Type, Features: Ironstone, plain white; cups without handles; decorated set has handles on the cups and garlands of flowers in purple and orange
Identical Blanks with Different Decorations: Two types are shown here; there is also a mulberry (marbled) set
Measurements: Teapot, 5½″; sugar, 4¾″; creamer, 3″; cup, 2″, saucer, 4¼″; waste bowl, 2¾″ tall and 3½″ across
Classification: Scarce
Collection: Lechler (ironstone plain); Strong Museum (partial decorated set)
Price Range for Complete Sets in Good Condition: $325.00 to 375.00
References or Author's Comments: The only reference to Barrow & Co. that this author could find was located in J.P. Cushion's *Handbook of Pottery & Porcelain Marks*, published by Faber & Faber, London. Boston.

Barrow & Co.'s Ironstone

Double Bands

Known Pattern Pieces: Tea set for six
Point of Origin, Date: Barrow & Co.; Fenton; This company was in business in 1855, although this author feels these sets are earlier. The set is marked Barrow & Co.

Known Pattern Pieces: Tea set
Point of Origin, Date England; circa 1840-60
Colors, Ware Type, Features: Earthenware with double ring trim; fancy handles
Identical Blanks with Different Decorations: Floral designs
Measurements: Child-size; teapot about 4″ tall
Classification: Scarce
Collection: Steffen
Price Range for Complete Sets in Good Condition: $150.00 to 175.00

*AMHERST JAPAN (correct name)

Known Pattern Pieces: Tea set
Point of Origin, Date: England
Colors, Ware Type, Features: Orange, cobalt and gold; marked "Amherst Japan" within a scroll and floral design; cups with ruffled rims and plain rims
Identical Blanks with Different Decorations: Flow Blue floral
Measurements: Teapot, 4¼″ tall; sugar, 2¾″ tall; creamer, 2¼″; cup, 1 ¾″ saucers, 4½″; plate, 5″; waste bowl, about 2¾″ tall and 4¼″ across
Classification: Very rare
Collection: Lechler
Price Range for Complete Sets in Good Condition: $1,000.00 to 1,500.00

Trellis

Known Pattern Pieces: Tea set with two servers; dinner set
Point of Origin, Date England; Copeland; 1860-1875; Copeland mark impressed in curved form
Colors, Ware Type, Features: Brown transfers of ivy covered trellis; pear-shaped teapot; handles on cups do not match teapot
Identical Blanks with Different Decorations: Dinner set may be seen in Milbourn, page 120; tea sets known plain with brown diamonds in ring; cobalt monochrome, slightly flowing
Measurements: Teapot, 4″; sugar, 3¼″; creamer, 2½″; cup, 2″; saucer, 4½″; serving plates, (2) 5″ x 5¼″; waste bowl, 2½ tall and 4¼″ across; (large tureen complete, 3½″ tall; gravy 2½″ long)
Classification: Obtainable
Collection: Lechler
Price Range for Complete Sets in Good Condition: $225.00 to 325.00

Green and White Seaweed

Known Pattern Pieces: Tea set (only two pieces shown here) dinner set shown later in English dinner sets
Point of Origin, Date: England; Charles Meigh & Son, Old Hall Pottery, Hanley, Staffordshire Potteries
Colors, Ware Type, Features: Earthenware; green seaweed type; bud finials
Measurements: Sugar, 3½″ tall; creamer, 2″ tall
Classification: Rare
Collection: Lechler
Price Range for Complete Sets in Good Condition: Tea set, $325.00 to 375.00
References or Author's Comments: These two pieces are shown in the dinner set section. I bought the dinner set as shown and didn't realize until after the picture was taken that the sugar and creamer didn't belong in that picture.

MATLOCK (correct name)

Known Pattern Pieces: Tea set
Point of Origin, Date: England
Colors, Ware Type, Features: Greek Key pattern circles the pieces of this stained and crazed English tea set
Measurements: Unavailable
Classification: Scarce
Collection: Steffen
Price Range for Complete Sets in Good Condition: $175.00 to 225.00

51

Plain Pink Bands

Known Pattern Pieces: Tea set with two pots
Point of Origin, Date: English; circa 1861-67
Colors, Ware Type, Features: Good porcelain with plain pink bands; teapot split handle; two pots
Identical Blanks with Different Decorations: See split-handle, Rick-rack Luster in this book; found also with hand painted butterflies; also with flowers
Measurements: Teapot, 4 1/16″, tall; pot, 5″; creamer, 2 3/4″; cup, 2 1/4″; saucer, 4 3/4″; plate, 6 1/4″; serving plate, 6 1/4″ handle to handle; waste bowl, 2 1/2″
Classification: Obtainable
Collection: Lechler
Price Range for Complete Sets in Good Condition: $145.00 to 200.00

Split-Handle, Rick-Rack Luster

Known Pattern Pieces: Tea set
Point of Origin, Date: England; attributed to Minton; circa 1860
Colors, Ware Type, Features: Dabs of pink, green and yellow with pink luster accent; two different blanks with same decoration shown in this publication; similar blanks also shown in this book; teapot has a split handle
Identical Blanks with Different Decorations: Butterflies; flowers; plain white with colored bands
Measurements: Teapot, 4 1/16″; sugar, 3 1/4″; creamer, 3″; cup, 2″; saucer, 4 1/4″; plate, 5″; waste bowl, 2 1/2″; basket (not purchased with set) 2 1/2″ x 4 1/2″; serving plate, 6 1/4″ handle to handle

Classification: Scarce
Collection: Lechler; partial set on table, Strong Museum
Price Range for Complete Sets in Good Condition: $150.00 to 325.00
References or Author's Comments: To see the rest of the set pictured on the tea table, look in the parlor section of this book. The rest of the set is on the sewing stand by the Lincoln rocker. Thomas Minton established the Minton pottery at Stoke-on-Trent in 1793. Early Minton is seldom marked, but after 1862, all items were marked. (The set shown here has no mark)

CHINTZ (correct name); also toy Ohio Bell phone

Known Pattern Pieces: Tea and dinner set
Point of Origin, Date: England; Ridgway; 1881
Colors, Ware Type, Features: Navy blue on white earthenware; butterflies, ferns and flowers; also comes in light blue, pink; green
Identical Blanks with Different Decorations: Maiden-Hair-Fern tea set and dinner set
Measurements: Teapot, 3 1/8″; sugar, 2 5/8″; creamer, 2″; cup, 1 1/4″; saucer, 3 1/2″ ; plate, 4 1/2″; waste bowl, 3 1/4″
Classification: Unusual in navy
Collection: Lechler; Ohio Bell phone Freshour collection
Price Range for Complete Sets in Good Condition: $300.00 to 325.00; phone, $50.00 to 100.00.
References or Author's Comments: Ohio Bell phone has "patented Feb. 24, 1914 Play System"; 10 1/2 long

Gold Clover Leaf

Known Pattern Pieces: Tea sets (two blanks, one design shown here)

Point of Origin, Date: England; circa 1868-1883

Colors, Ware Type, Features: Porcelain body with gold clover leaf on pieces and inside cups; sets come with a variety of different cups; this design predates traditional tea leaf; graceful lines on both sets

Measurements: Teapot, 3¼"; sugar, (wrong lid) 3"; creamer, 2½"; cup, 1¾"; saucer, 4¼"; plate, 5"; waste bowl, 2¼". Measurements for both sets are about the same. In fact, both sets were bought at the same time.

Classification: Scarce

Collection: Lechler; also Cedar Antiques

Price Range for Complete Sets in Good Condition: $200.00 to 225.00

References or Author's Comments: Bridgewood & Sons began in 1805 and their gold leaf design predates the traditional tea leaf. The same design, however, was produced by William Adams and Company.

POMPADORE (correct name)

Known Pattern Pieces: Tea set and coffee set

Point of Origin, Date: England; attributed by this author to Hollinshead and Kirkham (see reference below); circa 1870-1900

Colors, Ware Type, Features: Brown flowers on earthenware; pattern name written on base with "H & K"

Identical Blanks with Different Decorations: None shown in this book

Measurements: Teapot 3¼"; coffee pot, 5½"; sugar, 3½"; cup, 2"; saucer, 4¼"; plate, 4¼"; waste bowl, 2⅐" tall

Classification: Obtainable

Collection: Baugh

Price Range for Complete Sets in Good Condition: $150.00 to 200.00

References or Author's Comments: The mark "H & K" was also used by Hackwood and Keeling who did produce children's sets. However, I feel that this set's blanks are not as early as 1835-36.

Staffordshire Paneled Willow

53

Known Pattern Pieces: Tea set
Point of Origin, Date: England; circa 1873-1890; marked H.A. & Co.; attributed to H. Aynsley & Co. by English dealer
Colors, Ware Type, Features: Round teapot with six slated sides; earthenware
Measurements: Teapot, 4½″; open sugar or waste bowl, 2″ tall and 3″ across; creamer, 2″; cup, 1¾″; saucer, 4″ across
Classification: Rare
Collection: Lechler
Price Range for Complete Sets in Good Condition: $225.00 to 350.00
References or Author's Comments: Three companies used H.A. & Co.: Harvey Adam & Co. 1870-85 Longton; Henry Alcock & Co. 1861-1910, Colbridge; H. Aynsley & Co. Longton 1873-1932

English Blue Willow

Known Pattern Pieces: Tea set
Point of Origin, Date: England; circa 1882
Colors, Ware Type, Features: Plump ware with pointed finials; willow pattern in blue; one person on the bridge; pagoda
Measurements: Teapot, 5″; sugar, 4½″; creamer, 3¾″ spout to base; cup, 1¾;″ saucer, 4¾″; plate, 5¼″
Classification: Rare
Collection: Lechler
Price Range for Complete Sets in Good Condition: $250.00 to 325.00

Staffordshire Octagon Blue Willow

Known Pattern Pieces: Tea set
Point of Origin, Date: England; circa 1870-1880
Colors, Ware Type, Features: Available in rose, brown, green and blue with several different patterns on earthenware
Identical Blanks with Different Decorations: Mae; Girl and Dog; Spatter; Sponge; Stag; Oyster; Carnation; Dahlia; War Bonnet; Apple Blossom; Leafy; Water Hen; Punch and Judy; see, also *Children's Glass Dishes China and Furniture*, pages 24, 26, 138, 139
Measurements: Teapot, 5″; sugar, 4½″; creamer, 3¼; cup, 2″; saucer, 4¼″; plate, 5″
Classification: Unusual with willow on this blank
Collection: Lechler
Price Range for Complete Sets in Good Condition: $325.00 to 375.00

Staffordshire Spatterware

Known Pattern Pieces: Tea set for six
Point of Origin, Date: England
Colors, Ware Type, Features: Sponge (type) design in red; also known in blue, brown and black
Identical Blanks with Different Decorations: Water Hen; Stag; Mae; Punch and Judy; Apple Blossom; Blue Leafy; Child and Dog; Mae on the Step; Dahlia; Oyster; Wagon Wheel
Measurements: Teapot, 5″; sugar, 4½″; creamer, 3$^{1}/_{4}$″; cup, 2″; saucer, 4$^{1}/_{4}$″; plate, 5″
Classification: Rare
Collection: Lundquest
Price Range for Complete Sets in Good Condition: $425.00 to 600.00

Stick Spatter Staffordshire

Known Pattern Pieces: Tea set for six
Point of Origin, Date: England
Colors, Ware Type, Features: Earthenware with stick decorations in green, blue, red, brown
Identical Blanks with Different Decorations: Punch and Judy; Stag; Water Hen; Apple Blossom; Leafy; Mae; Mae on Steps
Measurements: Teapot, 5″; sugar, 4½″; creamer, 3⅛″; cup, 2″; saucer, 4½″; waste bowl, 2½″; plate, 5⅜″
Classification: Scarce
Collection: Lechler
Price Range for Complete Sets in Good Condition: $175.00 to 200.00
References or Author's Comments: Stick spatter is a term to identify a type of decoration which combines hand painting (at times) with transfer-painting. The spatter decoration was accomplished with a sponge, a brush, or a stick dabbed in paint. The majority of this ware was produced in England from 1850 to the late 1800's. It was also produced in Holland, France and America.

Known Pattern Pieces: Tea set
Point of Origin, Date: England; Staffordshire Potteries; marked "B.A. P.yC.yL."
Colors, Ware Type, Features: All over light blue with white flowers; earthenware, also known in brown
Measurements: Teapot, 4½″; sugar, 4″; cup, 2¼″; saucer, 4¼″; plate, 5″
Classification: Scarce in this shape
Collection: Lechler
Price Range for Complete Sets in Good Condition: $125.00 to 175.00
References or Author's Comments: The bulbous shape is more difficult to find than the slat-sided set with the same apple blossoms found on page 139 of *Children's Glass Dishes, China and Furniture*

PERSIAN

Known Pattern Pieces: Tea sets (shown on two different blanks)
Point of Origin, Date: England; Staffordshire Potteries; late 1800's
Colors, Ware Type, Features: Cobalt blue on white earthenware; oriental motif of fans, fish and other interesting design combinations
Identical Blanks with Different Decorations: Water Hen; Stag; Apple Blossom; Child and Dog; Blue Leafy; Punch and Judy; Spatter; Sponge
Measurements: Slat-sided set: teapot, 5″, sugar, 4½″; creamer, 3¼″; cup, 2″; saucer, 4¼″; plate, 5″. Puff-bottom set: teapot, 5¾″; plate, 5⅓; saucer, 4½″
Classification: Scarce
Collection: Gardner and Lechler
Price Range for Complete Sets in Good Condition: $125.00 to 225.00

Apple Blossom (Bulbous)

Derby White and Gold

Known Pattern Pieces: Tea set for six
Point of Origin, Date: England; circa 1890; Derby Porcelain Works, W. Duesbury, Bloor, Royal Crown Porcelain Co., Derby
Colors, Ware Type, Features: Excellent porcelain; graceful lines; gold trimmed; ruffled rims; marked Royal Crown Derby with crown, emblem and England
Measurements: Teapot, 5″; sugar, 4¼″; creamer, 2¼″; cup, 1¼″; saucer, 4¼″; waste bowl, 2¼″ tall and 4¼″ across; plates, 5″; (2) serving plates, 5¾″ x 6¼″
Classification: Uncommon
Collection: Lechler
Price Range for Complete Sets in Good Condition: $125.00 to 275.00
References or Author's Comments: For marking, see Godden's *Encyclopedia of British Pottery and Porcelain Marks,* page 203

Band of Pink Ovals and Diamonds

Known Pattern Pieces: Tea set
Point of Origin, Date: England; circa 1891-1900; Royal Worcester England; Rd. No. 449174
Colors, Ware Type, Features: Excellent porcelain with plain pink bands of ovals and diamonds; hand painted; gold accents
Measurements: Teapot, 4½″; sugar or waste bowl, 2¼″ tall and 3¼″ across; creamer, 2¼″; cup, 1³/₄″; saucer, 4½″; plate, 4½″
Classification: Uncommon
Collection: Lechler
Price Range for Complete Sets in Good Condition: $125.00 to 175.00

Cream with Brown Flowers

Known Pattern Pieces: Tea set for two
Point of Origin, Date: Europe; circa 1890-1900
Colors, Ware Type, Features: Light weight pottery-type ware; wonderful shapes with quality decorations
Measurements: Teapot, 4¼″; sugar, 3″; creamer, 2″; cup, 1¾″; saucer, 3¼″; plate, 4½″
Classification: Not often seen
Collection: Bobst
Price Range for Complete Sets in Good Condition: $175.00 to 200.00

Rib-Moulded Pink and White

Known Pattern Pieces: Tea set
Point of Origin, Date: Europe
Colors, Ware Type, Features: White quality porcelain with pink trim; rib-moulded design which tapers and flares toward the base
Measurements: Teapot, 4½″; creamer, 2¾″; cup, 2″; saucer, 4″; plate, 6″
Classification: Uncommon
Collection: Lechler
Price Range for Complete Sets in Good Condition: $225.00 to 325.00

Shell-Thin With Violets

Known Pattern Pieces: Tea set for six with spoons (found in original box)

Point of Origin, Date: Originally purchased in England from Vanheems & Wheeler, 47, Berners Street, Oxford St. London. W. The box was sent to Rev. E. Kynaston Burnham Sutton Rectory Kings Lynn

Colors, Ware Type, Features: Thin white crimped body trimmed with burnished gold and light blue violets; interesting shapes and sizes; ruffled rims on all pieces

Identical Blanks with Different Decorations: Possibly, but unknown to date

Measurements: Teapot, 4″ tall and 5½″ long from spout to handle; open sugar, 1½″ tall and 2¾″ across; creamer, 2¼″; cup, 1¾″ tall; saucer 4″ across; spoons, 2½″ long

Classification: Rare in original form

Collection: Lechler

Price Range for Complete Sets in Good Condition: $250.00 to 350.00

Known Pattern Pieces: Tea set

Point of Origin, Date: Late 1800's; European

Colors, Ware Type, Features: Pink and blue decorations with pink luster and gold trim

Measurements: Teapot, around 5½″ tall; cup, 2″; saucer, 4″; plate, 5″

Classification: Obtainable

Collection: Sembric

Price Range for Complete Sets in Good Condition: $75.00 to 125.00

ENGLISH TEA SETS, PEOPLE, ANIMALS

Children's Pastimes

Known Pattern Pieces: Tea set with two pots

Point of Origin, Date: England; circa 1830

Colors, Ware Type, Features: Earthenware, transfer-printed, red on white; two pots; children playing with hoop; doll, toy tea set, basket, houses, churches--all in background

Measurements: Unavailable

Classification: Very rare

Collection: Strong Museum, card catalogue number 81, 164

Price Range for Complete Sets in Good Condition: $400.00 to 500.00

Luster Trimmed Flowers

At The Well

Known Pattern Pieces: Tea set
Point of Origin, Date: England; Staffordshire Potteries; circa 1840-60
Colors, Ware Type, Features: Rose on white earthenware; two people (water sellers) at a well with steepled building in background; oriental appeal; cobalt E (type) mark on a few pieces; ring handles on three main pieces
Measurements: Teapot, 6″; sugar, 5¼″, creamer, 3½″, cup, 2″; saucer, 4¾″; plate, 5¼″
Classification: Scarce
Collection: Lechler
Price Range for Complete Sets in Good Condition: $150.00 to 225.00
References or Author's Comments: In the book *Staffordshire* by Petra Williams, there is a variation of At The Well called Grecian Font on page 283.

GIPSEY (correct name as shown on set)

Known Pattern Pieces: Tea set
Point of Origin, Date England; circa mid-1800's; attributed to Thompson and Co. by Milbourn
Colors, Ware Type, Features: Green, also known in rose; two maids at a back door having fortunes told; marked "Gipsey" in a cloud-like ellipse
Identical Blanks with Different Decorations: Possibly floral, also a scene of a lady riding side-saddle
Measurements: Teapot, 6″ long from spout to handle, 3¾″ tall (the handle is taller than the pot); creamer, 2½″; cup, 1¾″; saucer, 5″
Classification: Rare
Collection: Lechler
Price Range for Complete Sets in Good Condition: $350.00 to 390.00
References or Author's Comments: Milbourn refers to this set in *Understanding Miniature British Pottery and Porcelain* on pages 55 and 56

Oriental Youth

Known Pattern Pieces: Tea set
Point of Origin, Date: England; mid-1800's
Colors, Ware Type, Features: Earthenware; blue transfers; children with chinese bells; girl skipping rope; oriental musician; squash blossom finial
Measurements: Teapot, 3½″; sugar, 3″; creamer, 2″
Classification: Rare
Collection: Lundquest
Price Range for Complete Sets in Good Condition: $350.00 to 400.00

Girl With A Goat

Known Pattern Pieces: Tea set
Point of Origin, Date: England; circa 1871; attributed to Edge Malkin & Co.
Colors, Ware Type, Features: Earthenware with mulberry transfers; comes also in blue, brown or rose; lids have loop design; spout has a flower cluster; buildings in background
Measurements: Teapot, 4¼″ tall; sugar, 3¾″; creamer, 2½″; saucer, 5″; plate, 5″
Classification: Obtainable (mulberry coloring difficult to locate)
Collection: Lechler
Price Range for Complete Sets in Good Condition: $200.00 to 325.00
References or Author's Comments: Attributed to Edge Malkin & Co. by Petra Williams in *Staffordshire*, page 554.

Italian (correct name)

Known Pattern Pieces: Tea set
Point of Origin, Date: England; marked (curved) Copeland Spode's Italian England
Colors, Ware Type, Features: Blue transfer on white earthenware; seated person on right of teapot; person with staff and another on hands and knees by water, buildings in background
Measurements: Teapot, 3¼″
Classification: Very rare
Collection: Lechler
Price Range for Complete Sets in Good Condition: $450.00 to 550.00
References or Author's Comments: Spode's Italian pattern was introduced in 1816. It was to have been based on a drawing attributed to the Dutch artist named Frederick de Moucheron (1638-86). (See pages 191, 192 of Coysh and Henrywood's *The Dictionary of Blue and White Printed Pottery*).

*Woman by the Urn

Known Pattern Pieces: Tea set
Point of Origin, Date: England; circa 1850-1860
Colors, Ware Type, Features: Mulberry on earthenware; scenic background; woman by urn in a garden; dimity style border
Identical Blanks with Different Decorations: Brown transfers with hand painting in same basic design
Measurements: Teapots, 4¼″ tall; sugar, 3½″; cup, 1¾″; saucer, 4½″; waste bowl, 2¾″ tall
Classification: Rare
Collection: Lechler
Price Range for Complete Sets in Good Condition: $275.00 to 325.00

THE BOWER (correct name)

Known Pattern Pieces: Tea set; possibly dinner set
Point of Origin, Date: England; Edge Malkin & Co.; 1873-1903
Colors, Ware Type, Features: Rose transfers on earthenware; also in blue, sepia
Identical Blanks with Different Decorations: Chang; Pet Goat; Willow (tea and dinner set)
Measurements: Teapot, 3¾″; sugar, 3″; creamer, 2″; cup, 2¼″; saucer, 4¾″; plate, 5″; waste bowl, 2½″
Classification: Scarce
Collection: Lechler
Price Range for Complete Sets in Good Condition: $275.00 to 325.00

Farm

Known Pattern Pieces: Tea set for six
Point of Origin, Date: Scotland; David Methven & Sons; marked Imperial D.M. & Sons; 1840-1930; Kirkcaldy Pottery, Fife, Scotland
Colors, Ware Type, Features: Red or blue on earthenware; also known in brown; wonderfully complex transfers with vivid detail including two people with fringed hats talking with a seated person; donkey, farm and mill in distance
Measurements: Teapot, 3¼″; sugar, 2¾″; creamer, 2″; cup, 2″; saucer, 4¼″; waste bowl, 2″ tall and 3½″ across rim
Classification: Uncommon
Collection: Lechler
Price Range for Complete Sets in Good Condition: $375.00 to 400.00
References or Author's Comments: David Methven died in 1861. His work was continued by Andrew R. Young. Later products were marked "D.M. & S."

Known Pattern Pieces: Tea set; may also be a dinner set
Point of Origin, Date: England; Edge Malkin & Co. (possibly others); 1873-1903
Colors, Ware Type, Features: Black transfers on white earthenware; oriental design with two people and a leaning tree; known also in rose, sepia and blue
Identical Blanks with Different Decorations: The Bower; Pet Goat; Willow (tea and dinner sets)
Measurements: Teapot, 3¾″; sugar, 3″; creamer, 2″; cup, 2¼″; saucer, 4¾″; plate, 5″; waste bowl, 2½″
Classification: Scarce
Collection: Lechler
Price Range for Complete Sets in Good Condition: $275.00 to 325.00

Two On A Bridge Brown Willow

Known Pattern Pieces: Tea set
Point of Origin, Date: England
Colors, Ware Type, Features: Brown willow transfer on earthenware; some crazing
Measurements: Teapot, 4⅜″; creamer, 5¾″; cup, 2½″; saucer, 4⅛″; plate, 4″
Classification: Unusual in brown
Collection: Lechler
Price Range for Complete Sets in Good Condition: $225.00 to 275.00

*Birds and Holly

Known Pattern Pieces: Tea set with waste bowl and two underplates

Point of Origin, Date: Attributed to England

Colors, Ware Type, Features: Porcelain with high glaze; hand painted birds and holly; quality ware; green rim paint to match the holly leaves

Measurements: Teapot, 5″; sugar, 4½″; creamer, 3″; cup, 2⅛″; saucer, 4¼″; cake plates, 7″ handle to handle; waste bowl, 2¾″ tall and 3½″ across

Classification: Rare

Collection: Lechler

Price Range for Complete Sets in Good Condition: $265.00 to 400.00

Stag

Known Pattern Pieces: Tea set

Point of Origin, Date: England; circa 1870

Colors, Ware Type, Features: Rose, brown, blue, green; unusual shape; this design appears on several different Staffordshire shapes

Identical Blanks with Different Decorations: Water Hen; Mae, Girl and Dog; Spatter; Punch and Judy; see *Children's Glass Dishes, China and Furniture,* pages 138 and 139

Measurements: Teapot, 4¾″; sugar, 4⅛″; creamer, 2¼″; cup, 2″; saucer, 4¼″; waste bowl, 2¾″ tall; plate, 5″

Classification: More difficult to find this blank than the octagon shape

Collection: Lechler

Price Range for Complete Sets in Good Condition: $100.00 to 200.00

Mae With Apron

Known Pattern Pieces: Tea set for six

Point of Origin, Date: England; Charles Allerton and Sons, Park Works, Longton; 1880-1900

Colors, Ware Type, Features: Rose, brown, blue; earthenware

Identical Blanks with Different Decorations: Other decorations on this blank include: Water Hen, Stag, Apple Blossom, Child and Dog, Leafy, Punch and Judy, Wagon Wheel, Dahlia, War Bonnet, Oyster, Butterfly, Grape, Double Rose, Primrose, Single Rose, Urn, Spatter patterns.

Measurements: Teapot, 5″; sugar, 4½″; creamer, 3¼″; cup, 2″; saucer, 4¼″; plate, 5″; waste bowl, 2½″ tall

Classification: Common

Collection: Lundquest

Price Range for Complete Sets in Good Condition: $150.00 to 200.00

References or Author's Comments: See pages 138 and 139 of *Children's Glass Dishes, China and Furniture* for other decorations on this blank as well as other Blanks with this decoration. See, also, in this book: Persian and all over Staffordshire Spatterware.

Bye-Baby Bunting

Known Pattern Pieces: Tea set for four or six
Point of Origin, Date: England; circa 1893
Colors, Ware Type, Features: Vivid decals of the Bye-Baby Bunting lullaby; teapot has the baby in a circle of pigs; pictures are on the lids
Identical Blanks with Different Decorations: Yes, floral designs; these decals are also found on other blanks shown on page 192 in *Children's Glass Dishes, China and Furniture*; also in this book
Measurements: Teapot, 4¼"; sugar, 3¼"; creamer, 2½"; cup, 1½"; saucer, 3½"; plate, 4"; waste bowl, 1½"
Classification: Scarce on this blank
Collection: Lechler
Price Range for Complete Sets in Good Condition: $200.00 to 325.00

Bye-Baby

Known Pattern Pieces: Tea set
Point of Origin, Date: England; circa 1870-1890
Colors, Ware Type, Features: Earthenware with same decals as found on "Bye-Baby Bunting" in this book
Identical Blanks with Different Decorations: See page 192 of *Children's Glass Dishes, China and Furniture*; Mother Hubbard, Old King Cole, Gold Wedding Band, Nursery Tales
Measurements: Teapot, 4¼"; sugar, 4¼"; creamer, 4"; cup, 2½"; saucer, 5"; plate, 5¼"; waste bowl, 2½"
Classification: Obtainable
Collection: Lundquist
Price Range for Complete Sets in Good Condition: $150.00 to 210.00

To Market! To Market!

Known Pattern Pieces: Tea set
Point of Origin, Date: England; circa 1900-1930; marked "Made in England"
Colors, Ware Type, Features: Vivid decals on white glazed pieces; teapot shows a man and a pig with "To Market"; open sugar has "Goosey, Goosey Gander"
Measurements: Teapot, 4"; open sugar, 1¾"; creamer, 2¾"; cup, 1¾"; saucer, 4½"; plate, 5½"
Classification: Obtainable
Collection: Lechler
Price Range for Complete Sets in Good Condition: $125.00 to $150.00

IVANHOE (correct name)

Known Pattern Pieces: Tea set
Point of Origin, Date: "British Made IVANHOE"; 1900's
Colors, Ware Type, Features: Green transfers on earthenware; also known in rose, brown and possibly blue; man on horse with cottage scene in background; wonderfully detailed
Measurements: Teapot, 4¼"; creamer, 2¼"; cup, 2"; saucer, 4"; waste bowl, 1¾" tall and 3" across
Classification: Common, but very interesting transfers
Collection: Lechler
Price Range for Complete Sets in Good Condition: $125.00 to 175.00

English Dutch Pots

Known Pattern Pieces Chocolate and tea set
Point of Origin, Date: England; NEWLAND (impressed), Stoke-on-Trent, Staffordshire England
Colors, Ware Type, Features: D #2705 L on base, porcelain; vivid decals, little girl with blue dotted dress appears on the lid of the chocolate pot and on the teapot. (She reappears at least once on cups, saucers and plates)
Measurements: Chocolate Pot, 7½" tall; teapot, 4¾" tall

Classification: Uncommon blanks
Collection: Lechler
Price Range for Complete Sets in Good Condition: $125.00 to 225.00

Novelty Toby

Known Pattern Pieces: Teapot
Point of Origin, Date: England; circa 1929-42; marked "E S T (A) Allertons, made in England"
Colors, Ware Type, Features: Vivid painting, twig handle and spout
Measurements: Teapot, 3"
Classification: Common
Collection: Lechler
Price Range for Complete Sets in Good Condition: $45.00 to 75.00

ENGLISH DINNER AND DESSERT SETS

Lion's Heads

Known Pattern Pieces: Dinner set
Point of Origin, Date: England; circa 1820; possibly Leeds
Colors, Ware Type, Features: Lion Head finials on covered pieces in cobalt; cream-colored body with blue edges; earthenware; underglaze paint; feather-edge style
Classification: Very rare

Collection: Strong Museum
Price Range for Complete Sets in Good Condition: $1,000.00 to $2,000.00
References or Author's Comments: Strong Museum card catalogue numbers, 77.3058 and 77.3017

Brown Banded Soft Paste

Known Pattern Pieces: Dinner Set
Point of Origin, Date: Circa 1820-1840
Colors, Ware Type, Features: Cream-colored ware with brown bands
Measurements: Tureen shown in *Children's Glass Dishes, China and Furniture*, 1 ¾″ x 2¾″; remainder may be seen in Strong Museum
Classification: Very rare
Collection: Strong Museum
Price Range for Complete Sets in Good Condition: $400.00 to 600.00
References or Author's Comments: Strong Museum card catalogue number 77.3081; *Children's Glass Dishes, China and Furniture*, page 198

*Ferns and Flowers

Known Pattern Pieces: Dinner set in standard size and miniature
Point of Origin, Date: England; attributed to Charles Keeling (applied "C.K." impressed on a raised pad on a single piece of toy ware) 1822-1825
Colors, Ware Type, Features: Delicate, thin body with navy blue flowers and ferns flowing a bit
Identical blanks with different decorations: Copy of toy set in adult ware
Measurements: Plates: 3″, 4″; platters: 4″, 4¾″; tureens: 2¼″ tall and 4″ handle to handle, 3¼″ tall and 5½″ handle to handle; sauce, 1″ and 3¼″ handle to lip
Classification: Rare
Collection: Lechler
Price Range for Complete Sets in Good Condition: $325.00 to 400.00
References or Author's Comments: There is an adult set with the exact decorations and blank-style pieces.

Blue Willow

Known Pattern Pieces: Large dinner set
Point of Origin, Date: 1820-1830
Colors, Ware Type, Features: Willow pattern flowing; soft paste
Classification: Very rare
Collection: Strong Museum, card cat. no. 77.3088
Price Range for Complete Sets in Good Condition: $1,000.00 to 1,500.00

Wood's Willow

Known Pattern Pieces: Large dinner set
Point of Origin, Date: England; circa 1820-1840; impressed mark "Wood"
Colors, Ware Type, Features: Soft paste; vivid blues; different oriental scenes--some have two people on the bridge, one with a staff, some show a pagoda and willows; some of the blue flows outside determined lines
Measurements: Platters: 4½", 3½"; tureen, 2½"; covered vegetable base, 3¼" x 3¼"
Classification: Very rare
Collection: Lechler
Price Range for Complete Sets in Good Condition: $800.00 to 1,200.00

Laurel Leaves

Known Pattern Pieces: Dinner set
Point of Origin, Date: England; circa 1830-1840
Colors, Ware Type, Features: Soft paste; hand painted decorations; common size in dinner ware
Measurements: Unavailable; similar in size to Hackwood dinner sets
Classification: Rare
Collection: Strong Museum, card catalogue no. 77.3057
Price Range for Complete Sets in Good Condition: $500.00 to 700.00

English Scenes

Known Pattern Pieces: Large dinner set with twelve different English scenes
Point of Origin, Date: England; circa 1830
Colors, Ware Type, Features: Transfer printed earthenware; blue on white; scenic style
Identical blanks with different decorations: Unknown, picture name and picture placement; top dish is Abbey Mill; first plate in middle row is De Gaunt Castle; covered dish is Lechlade Bridge; last dish in middle row is Kenelworth; first row left is Abbey Mill; small plate in front row middle is Blaize castle; first row, far right, top platter is of Abbey Mill
Classification: Very rare
Collection: Strong Museum, card catalogue number 77.3085
Price Range for Complete Sets in Good Condition: $1,000.00 to 2,000.00
References or Author's Comments: The twelve (named) views found on this toy set are as follows: Bysham Monastery, St. Mary's Dover, Lanercost Priory, De Gaunt Castle, Donington Park, Entrance to Blaize Castle, Lechlade Bridge, Embdon Castle, Tewkesbury Church, Corf Castle, Kenelworth Priory, Abbey Mill

*Tower

Known Pattern Pieces: Large toy dinner set
Point of Origin, Date: England; Copeland and Garrett (Wm. Copeland was a partner in the Spode Works, Stoke, Staffordshire. Tower was a much used design during the period from 1820-1830) Copeland and Garrett are impressed; K appears on some; "New Blanche" appears in the center of each toy piece ("New Blanche" is the name used by Copeland and Garrett for their earthenware)
Colors, Ware Type, Features: Earthenware (called "New Blanche"); blue transfers on white; variants of the Tower pattern may be noted in *The Dictionary of Blue and White Printed Pottery* by Coysh; identical blanks with different decorations. The Tower border may also be seen on Spode's Milkmaid design. Milkmaid is another famous Spode pattern
Measurements: Soups, 3¼" across; pudding plates, 2½"; plates, 3", 2 15/16"; platters: (2) 4", 5", 5½"; (2) covered vegetables, 2" tall and 3" across. There are many more pieces to this set.
Classification: Very rare
Collection: Lechler
Price Range for Complete Sets in Good Condition: $1,000.00 to 2,000.00
References or Author's Comments: The Tower pattern is based on the engraving showing the Bridge of Salaro around Porta Salara from Merigot's *Views of Rome and Its Vicinity*.

Monopteros

Known Pattern Pieces: Dinner set
Point of Origin, Date: England; Rogers; circa 1820-1830
Colors;, Ware Type,; features: Light weight; biscuit-colored body; white slip with blue transfer printing; shows an ox and traveler in a medieval setting
Identical blanks with different decorations: Oriental scenes
Measurements: Large tureen, 3 13/16″ tall; plates, 2″, 3½″
Classification: Very rare in completion
Collection: Strong Museum; see card catalogue no. 77.3589
Price Range for Complete Sets in Good Condition: $1,000.00 to 2,000.00
References or Author's Comments: "Monopteros" is named from T. & W. Daniell's "Oriental Scenery and Views in Hindoostan" See Coysh, page 250 and 252, *Dictionary of Blue and White Printed Pottery 1780-1880,* See also Milbourn's *Understanding Miniature British Pottery and Porcelain*

*Hackwood's Blue Willow

Known Pattern Pieces: Dinner set
Point of Origin, Date: England; Hackwood; circa 1827-1843; impressed Hackwood
Colors, Ware Type, Features: Willow pattern on white soft paste
Identical blanks with different decorations: Monastery Hill (or Institution)
Measurements: Platters: (3) at 3¼″, 3½″, 4″, 4½″, (2) 5¼″, 5½″; plates: 2¾″, 3″, 3¼″, 3½″; soups, 3½″; covered vegetable (2) at 2″, 2¾″ across; tureens: 2½″, 3¾″; ladles, 2¾″, 3¾″; open salad, 1″ tall, 2½″ x 2½″; oval vegetable, (2) 1½″ tall and 3¼″ long; oval open vegetable, ½″ tall and 3¾″ long
Classification: Very rare in completion
Collection: Lechler
Price Range for Complete Sets in Good Condition: $1,000.00 to 1,500.00
References or Author's Comments: Reference is *Dictionary of Blue and White Printed Pottery* by Coysh and Henrywood and Petra Williams's *Staffordshire*

*Institution or Monastery Hill

Known Pattern Pieces: Large dinner set
Point of Origin, Date: England; Hackwood; circa 1827-1843
Colors, Ware Type, Features: Border of lillies, foliage and morning glories; center shows a person, a cow and a large institutional type building in the background; blue transfer on soft paste
Identical blanks with different decorations: Blue willow is on this blank

Measurements: Platters: (2) at 3¼″, 3½″, 4″, 4½″; (2) at 5¼″, 5½″; plates: 2¾″, 3″, 3¼″, 3½″; soups, 3½″; covered vegetables; (2) at 2″, 2¾″ across; tureens, 2½″, 3¾″; ladles, 2¾″, 3¾″; open salad, 1″ tall and 2½″ x 2½″; oval vegetable, (2) at 1½″ tall and 3¼″ long

Classification: Very rare in completion

Collection: Lechler

Price Range for Complete Sets in Good Condition: $1,500 to 2,000.00

References or Author's Comments: The Blue Willow set by Hackwood may also be seen in this publication.

English Oriental

Known Pattern Pieces: Dinner set (large)

Point of Origin, Date: England; circa 1830-1860

Colors, Ware Type, Features: Earthenware; terra-cotta borders; each toy place setting has a different center with the borders carrying the same design throughout; themes: one man on bridge with large blossom in the sky; bridge with dirt and branches; berry bush; pagoda and heart tree; bridge and gazebo; large orange blossom; large pink blossom; bridge with two people; colors are orange, rose, black, green and terra-cotta

Measurements: Plates: 2″, 2½″, 3″, 3¾″; soups, 3¾″ and ¾″ deep

Classification: Very rare

Collection: Lechler

Price Range for Complete Sets in Good Condition: $500.00 to 800.00

*Garden Sports (correct title)

Known Pattern Pieces Tea and dinner sets

Point of Origin, Date: England; circa 1842; possibly Minton (see reference below)

Colors, Ware Type, Features: Blue transfers on earthenware; two children collecting what looks like eggs; two girls, one with a leash and one holding the animal still; two children with wheelbarrow

Identical Blanks with Different Decorations: Unknown

Measurements: Plates: 2¾″, 3½″, 4⅛″; soups, 4¼″; sauce boat, 2″ tall; long open vegetable, (2), 3″; crimped (inward) rimmed server, very unusual, footed, 3½″ long and 1¾″ tall; nest of platters: (2) 6″, 5¾″, 5″, 4¾″; scroll-handled platters: 4¾″, (2) 4¼″

Classification: Very rare

Collection: Lechler

Price Range for Complete Sets in Good Condition: $1,000.00 to 1,500.00

References or Author's Comments: Impressed mark such as found on the base of most of these set members is seen on page 440, first square under 1842 in Godden's *Encyclopedia of British Pottery and Porcelain Marks*.

*Copper Luster Tea Leaf (variant)

Known Pattern Pieces Large dinner set
Point of Origin, Date: England; 1835-1849
Colors, Ware Type, Features: Copper luster on white earthenware; artistic license caused a variation in the design, making it a three petal design with leaves
Identical Blanks with Different Decorations: Asiatic Birds (Flow Blue); navy blue with no flow; pastels
Measurements: Tureens: (2) 3¼", 4½"; plates: 3¼", 2½"; platters: 5¾" and (2) 4½" with scrolled handles, 4", 5½"; covered oval dishes, (2) at 2½"; open vegetable, 3½"
Classification: Rare with Tea Leaf and Flow Blue Asiatic Birds
Collection: Janet and Gale Fredrick
Price Range for Complete Sets in Good Condition: $800.00 to 1,000.00
References or Author's Comments: Tea Leaf is a decoration of copper or gold tea leaf sprigs placed on light weight stone china. It was first produced by Anthony Shaw of Longport, England, around 1850. By the late 1800's, other potters in Staffordshire produced this popular product, much of which came to the United States. There are several variations in design.

*Asiatic Birds

Known Pattern Pieces Large dinner set
Point of Origin, Date: England; Charles Meigh; circa 1835-1849
Colors, Ware Type, Features: Flow Blue; also, navy blue sets that do not flow; brown; pastels; earthenware
Identical Blanks with Different Decorations: Copper luster Tea Leaf (Variant) in this publication
Measurements: Platters: 4¼", 4½"; 5½"; soups, 3½"; tureen platters: 4¼", 4½", 5½", 5¾"; plates: 3", 3¼", 3¾", 2½"; two covered dishes: 2¾", 2½"; tureens: 3¼", 3½", 4¼"; two sauces, (2) 1¼"; open vegetable, 4½"; ladles: 3", 3½", 4½"
Classification: Very rare in Flow Blue (complete); also rare with Tea Leaf
Collection: Lechler
Price Range for Complete Sets in Good Condition: Flow Blue, $1,800.00 to 2,000.00

*Forget-Me-Not Flow Blue

Known Pattern Pieces: Dinner set
Point of Origin, Date: England; circa 1850
Colors, Ware Type, Features: Cobalt flowers and ferns flowing outside patterned lines; earthenware; impressed B, impressed O, also a cobalt design
Measurements: Plates: 3¼", 2¾", 3¾"; soups, 3¾" across and 1¾" tall; platters: (2) 6¼", 5¼", 5", 4¾" long; tureen platters, 5" long, 4" long; sauce, 2"; open vegetable (3) 4¼"; odd servers in leaf shape, (2) 2¾" long and 2¼" wide; tureens, 4" tall, (2) 3" tall; covered vegetable, 2½" tall and 4½" from open handle to open handle
Classification: Very rare
Collection: Private
Price Range for Complete Sets in Good Condition: $1,000.00 to 2,300.00
References or Author's Comments: All toy sets with the "Flow Blue" treatment are rare and sought with zeal

Slant Stripe Border

Known Pattern Pieces: Dinner set
Point of Origin, Date: England; circa 1830-1859
Colors, Ware Type, Features: Soft paste; light blue border with white slanted stripes; unusual addition is a meat platter with rivulets for drainage

Identical blanks with different decorations: Sets with different border decorations and colors
Measurements: Platters: 2½″, 3″, 4″, 5″, 5¾″; meat platter with drainage 5″ (also has standing bars on base); covered dishes, 3″; small tureen, 3½″; tureen platters: 5¼″, (2) 4½″ handle to handle; sauce, 1½″; plates: 2¾″, 3½″, 4¼″
Classification: Rare
Collection: Lechler
Price Range for Complete Sets in Good Condition: $325.00 to 600.00

MYRTLE WREATH (correct name)

Known Pattern Pieces: Dinner set
Point of Origin, Date: England; marked "J.M. & S."; circa 1841-1897; see reference or Author's Comments
Colors, Ware Type, Features: Slip-decorated earthenware; green and white transfer printing on soft paste; transfer printed wreath of leaves and borders of geometric design in dark green print
Classification: Rare
Collection: Strong Museum, card catalogue number 77.3076
Price Range for Complete Sets in Good Condition: $325.00 to 600.00
References or Author's Comments: J.M. & S. marks were used by the following: Job Meigh & Son, 1812-34; John Meir & Son, Turnstall, 1841-97; John Maddock, Burslem, 1855-69. This author considers 1812-34 too early for this particular set (reference, see Godden, page 725)

Calico

Known Pattern Pieces: Dinner set (30 pieces known)
Point of Origin, Date: England; circa 1835-1849; possibly Charles Meigh
Colors, Ware Type, Features: Sheet pattern print of brown calico
Identical blanks with different decorations: Other floral patterns; could be the same set of blanks as Asiatic Birds and Copper Luster Tea Leaf shown in this book
Classification: Scarce
Collection: Steffen
Price Range for Complete Sets in Good Condition: $325.00 to 375.00

Chelsea or Granny's Pattern

Known Pattern Pieces: Dinner set
Point of Origin, Date: England; circa 1850-1860
Colors, Ware Type, Features: White ware with raised blue design
Classification: Rare
Collection: Steffen
Price Range for Complete Sets in Good Condition: $300.00 to 400.00

Leaf Border in Mulberry

Known Pattern Pieces: Dinner Set
Point of Origin, Date: England; impressed W; impressed U; painted V
Colors, Ware Type, Features: Mulberry leaves strung around the border of each piece; earthenware
Measurements: Platters: 4¾″, 5½″, 6½″; plates: 2½″, 3″, 4″; soup, 3¾″; tureen, 4½″

Classification: Rare
Collection: Lechler
Price Range for Complete Sets in Good Condition: $275.00 to 400.00
References or Author's Comments: Impressed marks were made by applying a metal die to the items before firing

Dimmock's Green Loops

Known Pattern Pieces: Large dinner set
Point of Origin, Date: England; circa 1828-1859; Thomas Dimmock (Junr) & Co., Albion St.; Staffordshire Potteries
Colors, Ware Type, Features: Earthenware, white body with hunter green loops
Identical Blanks with Different Decorations: Other simple decorations
Measurements: Plates: 4″, 3½″, 3¼″; soup, 4″; open server, 2¼″; sauce, 1½″; covered servers, (2) 2½″; tureens; 3½″ (2), 4½″; deep open bowl, 4½″; platters (2), 5″ long; handled platters, 4½″, 5½″; shallow open platters, (2) 4½″, 5¼″
Classification: Uncommon
Collection: Lechler
Price Range for Complete Sets in Good Condition: $325.00 to 425.00
References or Author's Comments: See Godden's *Encyclopedia of British Pottery and Porcelain Marks*, page 208, monogram mark

AMADEUS (correct name)

Known Pattern Pieces: Dinner set
Point of Origin, Date: England; Hanley, Staffordshire; 1861-1886
Colors, Ware Type, Features: White Indian Stone China with blue border trim
Identical Blanks with Different Decorations: Various border trims
Measurements: Plates: 3″, 3″, 3½″; platters: 3¾″, 4″, 4½″, 5″, 5½″; soup, 3¾″; sauce, 2″; tureens: 4″, 4½″; vegetable dish, 4¾″; sauce boat, 1³/₄″
Classification: Scarce
Collection: Lundquest
Price Range for Complete Sets in Good Condition: $225.00 to 325.00
References or Author's Comments: Old Hall Indian Stone China was an impressed mark used by Charles Meigh and continued by Old Hall Earthenware Co., Ltd. The Old Hall Earthenware Co., Ltd. was a Staffordshire pottery.

Dimity: *Seaweed with Arrows; Delicate Seaweed

Known Pattern Pieces: Dinner sets
Point of Origin, Date: England; Charles Meigh & Son, Old Hall Pottery, Hanley, Staffordshire Potteries; circa 1851-1861
Colors, Ware Type, Features: Dimity dinner set comes in green or brown. The Dimity set is soft paste and marked Old Hall Indian Stone China; Seaweed with Arrows dinner set is green on white earthenware; Delicate Seaweed is found in blue on white earthenware. All sets may be found in other colors.
Identical Blanks with Different Decorations: Described above
Measurements: Tureens: 3¼″, 3½″, 5″, 5¼″; ladles: 3″, 3½″; open compote, 2½″; covered servers (2) 2½″; platters: 3″, 3½″, 4¼″, 5″, 5¾″; soup, 3¾″; open vegetable: 3″, 3¼″; plates: 2¼″, 2½″, 3″, 3¾″ 4″; sauce, (2) 1¾″; tureen platters: 4½″, 5″; servers, (2) 2½″ x 3¼″
Classification: Rare in completion
Collection: Lechler
Price Range for Complete Sets in Good Condition: $375.00 to 500.00
References or Author's Comments: Stone China is a name for hard, dense ceramic bodies introduced about 1805 by Josiah Spode II. This title is used for strong, ironstone type bodies such as the Seaweed with Arrows and the Delicate Seaweed. The words "Old Hall Indian Stone China", however, appear on the delicately potted Dimity set which appears to be soft paste and earlier than the other two.

Known Pattern Pieces: Dinner set
Point of Origin, Date: England
Colors, Ware Type, Features: Hand decorated earthenware
Classification: Rare
Collection: Strong Museum, catalogue card number 81.251
Price Range for Complete Sets in Good Condition: $500.00 to 600.00

FISHERS (correct name)

Known Pattern Pieces: Dinner set
Point of Origin, Date: England; 1860-1871; marked C. E. & M. (Cork, Edge and Malkin) Newport Pottery, Burslem; Staffordshire Potteries
Colors, Ware Type, Features: Earthenware; in green; also comes in other colors--blue, rose, mulberry; acorn finials
Identical Blanks with Different Decorations: Very much like Dimity, Seaweed with Arrows and Delicate Seaweed, all shown in this publication
Measurements: Plates: 2¼″, 2½″, 3½″, 3¾″; platters: 3″, 3½″, 4¼″, 5″, 5¾″, 6″; open compote, 2½″ tall, 5″; soup, 3¾″.
Classification: Rare
Collection: Lechler
Price Range for Complete Sets in Good Condition: $325.00 to 450.00

Child's Variety

Known Pattern Pieces: Dinner set
Point of Origin, Date: England; circa 1860
Colors, Ware Type, Features: Earthenware decorated with childish delights--animals, music, fruit
Identical Blanks with Different Decorations: Floral decorations; Seaweed decorations
Measurements: Tureen, 5″ tall
Classification: Rare in completion
Collection: Lechler
Price Range for Complete Sets in Good Condition: $425.00 to 525.00

Known Pattern Pieces: Dinner set
Point of Origin, Date: England; circa 1860
Colors, Ware Type, Features: Brown flowers on earthenware
Measurements: Covered tureen, 5″; gravy boat with attached underplate, 2¼″ x 4½″; platter, 6¼″; oval plate, 3¾″; plates: 4″, 5¼″
Classification: Scarce
Collection: Lundquest
Price Range for Complete Sets in Good Condition: $350.00 to 375.00

Copeland Blue and Gold

Known Pattern Pieces: Dinner set
Point of Origin, Date: England; circa 1850 to 1870
Colors, Ware Type, Features: Underglaze blue lines; gold trim on earthenware
Identical Blanks with Different Decorations: Same set decorated with rows of hearts in blue
Measurements: Open server, 4½″ x 4½″; plate, 4¾″; soup, 4½″; sauce, 2½″ x 4¼″; tureen, 4¼″ x 5½″; open server, 5¾″
Classification: Scarce
Collection: Lechler
Price Range for Complete Sets in Good Condition: $175.00 to 200.00
References or Author's Comments: The Copeland set with hearts may be seen in Milbourn's book on page 120.

*Chinese Red and Cobalt

Known Pattern Pieces: Dinner set
Point of Origin, Date: England; impressed circle, impressed "J"
Colors, Ware Type, Features: Chinese red and cobalt flora and feather designs with two unusual shell (type) servers
Measurements: Plates: 2¾″, 3¾″, 2⅛″; sauce boat, 2″; soup, 4⅛″; shell (shaped) servers (2), 3″ long; tureens: 3¼″, 2¼″; two lids to covered dishes, 3⅛″ across lid rim
Classification: Rare
Collection: Lechler
Price Range for Complete Sets in Good Condition: $500.00 to 800.00

*Pearl Dessert Set

Floral Staffordshire

Known Pattern Pieces: Dessert set
Point of Origin, Date: England; Burgess & Leigh; Hill Pottery; circa 1867-1889; marked "Pearl" with a beehive; Alcock also used the beehive marking
Colors, Ware Type, Features: Colored variety of flowers in yellow, green, orange, blue and red
Identical Blanks with Different Decorations: Gray and black scenic motif
Measurements: Compote, 3¼" tall and 5½" handle to handle; oval servers (2) 5" long; plates, 3¾"; servers, (2) 4¼" handle to handle; plate, scalloped with two handles, 4⅝"
Classification: Rare
Collection: Lechler
Price Range for Complete Sets in Good Condition: $175.00 to 325.00
References or Author's Comments: See Godden's *Encyclopedia of British Pottery and Porcelain Marks*, pages 116, 117

Fruit and Dessert Set

Known Pattern Pieces: Dessert set with two compotes
Point of Origin, Date: England; circa 1890
Colors, Ware Type, Features: Earthenware; apples, blueberries and blossoms on one compote; peaches, purple berries and blossoms on other compote; blue rims; gold trim; plates have different centers; green grapes, purple grapes, plums, blackberries
Measurements: Compotes, 2¾" tall and 4" across; plates are 2¾" across
Classification: Rare
Collection: Lechler
Price Range for Complete Sets in Good Condition: $125.00 to 150.00

Edge Malkin Blue Willow

Known Pattern Pieces: Dinner set
Point of Origin, Date: England; circa 1873-1903; Edge Malkin & Co., Newport and Middleport Potteries, Burslem, Staffordshire Potteries
Colors, Ware Type, Features: Brown Willow and Blue Willow earthenware dinner sets
Measurements: Plates: 3", 2¼"
Classification: Rare
Collection: Lechler
Price Range for Complete Sets in Good Condition: $450.00 to 525.00

Black Willow Wedgwood

Known Pattern Pieces: Dinner set
Point of Origin, Date: England; Wedgwood; January, 1876
Colors, Ware Type, Features: Black Willow; earthenware; Wedgwood impressed on bases; series of letters denotes year it was produced
Measurements: Soup, 3½"; plate, 3½"; platter, 3¾" long
Classification: Very rare
Collection: Lechler
Price Range for Complete Sets in Good Condition: $500.00 to 1,000.00

Blue Daisy

Known Pattern Pieces: Dinner set
Point of Origin, Date: Circa 1880; possibly Ridgway
Colors, Ware Type, Features: Light blue daisy transfers on earthenware
Identical Blanks with Different Decorations: Floral

Measurements: Plates: 3⅝", 4½"; soup, 4½"; tureen, 4½"; platters: 4½", 5½" 6", 7¼", 8"; sauce, 2½"; under plates: 5", 6⅞", 4⅝"
Classification: Obtainable
Collection: Lechler
Price Range for Complete Sets in Good Condition: $135.00 to 175.00

CHINTZ (correct name); MAIDEN HAIR FERN (correct name)

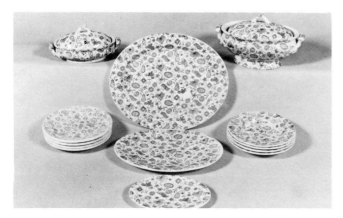

Known Pattern Pieces: Large dinner sets; tea sets
Point of Origin, Date: England; Ridgway; Stoke-on-Trent (both sets)
Colors, Ware Type, Features: Earthenware; Chintz design is busy and all over the ware; Maiden Hair Fern has Ginko (style) leaves
Measurements: Platters: 8", 7¼", 6"; plates: 3⅝", 4½"; casserole, 5¼"; tureens: 6⅜", 4⅛"; underplates: 5", 6⅞", 4⅝"; soup, 4½"
Classification: Obtainable
Collection: Lechler
Price Range for Complete Sets in Good Condition: $225.00 to 325.00

ROSAMOND (correct name)

Known Pattern Pieces: Dinner set
Point of Origin, Date: England; Bishop and Stonier; 1891-1900
Colors, Ware Type, Features: Semi-porcelain; swirled, melon ribbing; Rosamond has the Flow Blue treatment
Identical Blanks with Different Decorations: Blue or green willow; violets; children and toys
Measurements: Tureens: 4½", 5½", 6½"; platters: 4½", (2) 5½"; sauce, 2½"; plates: 3⅝", 4½"; soup, 4½"; ladle, 4"
Classification: Rare in Flow Blue; obtainable and desirable in other patterns
Collection: Lechler
Price Range for Complete Sets in Good Condition: $300.00 to 500.00
References or Author's Comments: Caduceus, the staff carried by Mercury, the messenger of the gods, is found on some Bishop and Stonier pieces.

Bishop and Stonier's Blue Willow

Known Pattern Pieces: Dinner set
Point of Origin, Date: England; Bishop and Stonier; 1891-1900
Colors, Ware Type, Features: Blue Willow transfer on white semi-porcelain; melon ribbing
Identical Blanks with Different Decorations: Green Willow; Rosamond (flowing blue flowers); Bishop and Stonier's children
Measurements: Tureens: 4½", 5½", 6½"; platters: 4½" (2), 5½"; sauce, 2½"; plates: 3⅝", 4½"; soup, 4½"; ladle, 4"
Classification: Obtainable and desirable

Collection: Lechler
Price Range for Complete Sets in Good Condition: $225.00 to 400.00
References or Author's Comments: The designs and their treatment help to tell the price of this set. If the set leans to flowing blue, the price goes up. (See also in this publication: Rosamond and Bishop and Stonier's Children)

Bishop and Stonier's Children

Known Pattern Pieces: Dinner set
Point of Origin, Date: England; Bishop and Stonier; 1891-1900
Colors, Ware Type, Features: Semi-porcelain; swirled body; vivid pictures of children and toys--children on a log, boy with finger in his mouth; train on a tureen lid, children in a field
Identical Blanks with Different Decorations: See in this publication: Blue Willow, Rosamond. There is also a set with violets which is not shown here.
Measurements: Tureens: 4½″, 5½″, 6½″; platters: 4½″ (2) 5¹/₂″; sauce, 2¹/₂″; plates: 3⁵/₈″, 4¹/₂″; soup, 4½″; ladle, 4″
Collection: Rare in Flow Blue; obtainable and desirable in other designs
Price Range for Complete Sets in Good Condition: $175.00 to 225.00

Shell Ware Willow

Known Pattern Pieces: Dinner set for six
Point of Origin, Date: England; 1900's; marked "shell ware" with a picture of a shell and "England, old English"; some pieces are also marked "Made in England"
Colors, Ware Type, Features: Earthenware with willow design; three people on the bridge, boat and pagoda
Identical Blanks with Different Decorations: Pagodas
Measurements: Platters: 7⅛″, 6⅛″, 5⅛″; covered dish, 5½″; plates: 4½″, 3⅞″; sauce, 1¾″
Classification: Scarce
Collection: Lechler
Price Range for Complete Sets in Good Condition: $175.00 to 225.00

Patchwork

Known Pattern Pieces: Dinner set
Point of Origin, Date: Occupied Japan; 1900's
Colors, Ware Type, Features: Porcelain; excellent decorations using cobalt, gold, chinese red
Measurements: Platter, 5¼″; covered tureen, 5¾″ tall and 5″ long
Classification: Unusual
Collection: Lechler
Price Range for Complete Sets in Good Condition: $200.00-275.00

*RHODESIA (correct name)

Known Pattern Pieces: Tea set; dinner set
Point of Origin, Date: England; Ridgway; circa 1900-1915
Colors, Ware Type, Features: Haviland (style) flowers in delicate clusters with blue ribbons; some crazing
Identical Blanks with Different Decorations: Humphrey's Clock; also Roses With Navy--both shown in this publication: some covered pieces have open finials and some are closed

Measurements: Teapot, 4½"; open sugar, 1¾" tall and 3" across; creamer, 2½"; cup, 1½"; saucer, 4"; waste bowl, 2⅛" tall and 3½" across; open ruffled bowl, 1¾" tall; two covered servers: 2½" and 3½"; nest of platters: 8", 7", 6¼", 5"; plates: 4½"; 3¾"; soup, 3¾"

Classification: Scarce

Collection: Lechler

Price Range for Complete Sets in Good Condition: $500.00 to 625.00

References or Author's Comments: The price for this set is high because of all the delicate pieces. If a complete set is found and in good condition. the price would be high. Note the finials on the covered pieces. The author has both closed and open finials within a Humphrey's Clock dinner set.

37

HUMPHREY'S CLOCK (correct name)

Known Pattern Pieces: Large tea and dinner set

Point of Origin, Date: England; Ridgway; W.R. S. & Co., Church Works; 1890-1908; marked in blue "Humphrey's Clock" in a banner and "England" is under the banner; a picture of the clock is shown

Colors, Ware Type, Features: Blue transfers (flows a bit) on earthenware; scenes of children and dogs playing and strolling in a park scene

Identical Blanks with Different Decorations: Rhodesia and Roses With Navy shown in this book

Measurements: Teapot, 4½"; sugar (open) 1½"; creamer, 1¾"; cup, 1¾"; saucer, 4¼"; open compote, 4½" across and 1¼" tall; waste bowl, 2⅛" tall and 3½" across; nest of platters: 8", 7", 6¼", 5"; plates: 4¼", 3¾"; soups, 3¾"; open ruffled bowl, 1¾" (2) covered servers: 2½", 3½"; also a very large covered dish not shown

Classification: Rare in completion

Collection: Lechler

Price Range for Complete Sets in Good Condition: Complete tea and dinner set combination, $500.00 to 600.00. Tea set alone and complete, $350.00 to 375.00; dinner set alone and complete, $350.00 to 390.00

References or Author's Comments: The author has both closed and open finials on the covered pieces within the set.

76

Known Pattern Pieces: Tea set
Point of Origin, Date: Germany; circa 1850
Colors, Ware Type, Features: Cut and applied flowers on porcelain; pastel colors
Measurements: Teapot, 3½"; cup, 1"; saucer, 2¾"
Classification: Rare
Collection: Lechler
Price Range for Complete Sets in Good Condition: $350.00 to 500.00
References or Author's Comments: A set such as this would be considered cabinet (show) ware

Storks

Known Pattern Pieces: Dinner set
Point of origin, date England; 1900's; marked "Made In England"
Colors, Ware Type, Features: Black silhouettes, trees, water and buildings trimmed in gold; crazing
Measurements: Platters: 5½", 6", 7"; (2) sauces, 2" lip to base; tureens, (2) 2½" tall; plates: 4½", 5½"
Classification: Difficult to locate
Collection: Lechler
Price Range for Complete Sets in Good Condition: $150.00 to 250.00

GERMAN TEA SETS, FLOWERS, BANDS AND SCENIC STRUCTURES

Applied Flowers

Floral Cabaret Set

Known Pattern Pieces: Tea set for two
Point of Origin, Date: Attributed to Dresden; raised "cross" marks the bases of some of the pieces
Colors, Ware Type, Features: Pearl skin with cut and applied flowers in blue with gold or pink with gold; quality production; light weight
Measurements: Tray, 8¼" x 9⅝"; teapot, 4¾"; sugar, 3"; creamer, 2½"; cup, 2⅛"; saucer, 4"
Classification: Obtainable
Collection: Lechler
Price Range for Complete Sets in Good Condition: $200.00 to 250.00

Indigo Flowers in Relief

Known Pattern Pieces: Tea set
Point of Origin, Date: Germany; 1898-1900
Colors, Ware Type, Features: White body with indigo trim; flowers cut out and hand applied; fish scale runners from top to base

Measurements: Teapot, 5″; sugar, 2½″; creamer, 2¾″; cup, 2½″
Classification: Rare
Collection: Lechler
Price Range for Complete Sets in Good Condition: $275.00 to 375.00
References or Author's Comments: Three members of the Schlegelmilch family produced porcelain in Germany in the nineteenth and early twentieth centuries. Their work is called: RS Prussia, RS Germany, RS Poland or RS Tillowitz. This author attributes the "Indigo Flowers in Relief" to RS Germany as a Schlegelmilch product.

Footed RS Prussia

Known Pattern Pieces: Tea set
Point of Origin, Date: Germany; 1898-1908
Colors, Ware Type, Features: Quality porcelain with graceful lines; pastel floral clusters; light blue background with pink and cream roses; gold trim
Identical Blanks with Different Decorations: Teapot without feet shown in *Children's Glass Dishes, China and Furniture* on page 159
Measurements: Teapot, 4″; creamer, 3¼″; cup, 1¼″; saucer, 2¾″; plate, 2¾″
Classification: Rare
Collection: Lechler
Price Range for Complete Sets in Good Condition: $350.00 to 400.00
References or Author's Comments: The Schlegelmilch family's work is referred to as: RS Prussia, RS Germany, RS Poland or RS Tillowitz. Erdmann Schlegelmilch founded a factory in Suhl, Thuringia, between 1861 and 1925. Reinhold established a factory in Tillowitz, Silesia, between 1869 and 1917. Oscar, a nephew began his business in Langewiesen, Thuringia, circa 1892 to 1950.

Scales

Known Pattern Pieces: Tea set (probably for two)
Point of Origin, Date: European
Colors, Ware Type, Features: Golden scales with blue dots accent on porcelain; unusual fish tail (type) handles
Measurements: Teapot, 4½″; sugar, 2½″; creamer, 2½″; cup, 1½″; saucer, 3½″
Classification: Scarce
Collection: Baugh
Price Range for Complete Sets in Good Condition: $100.00 to 200.00

Pink Luster with Gold Trim

Known Pattern Pieces: Tea set for four
Point of Origin, Date: European; no marking
Colors, Ware Type, Features: Floral design with pink luster and gold accents
Identical Blanks with Different Decorations: Other floral designs
Measurements: Teapot, 6½″; sugar, 5″; creamer, 4½″
Classification: Obtainable
Collection: Schmoker
Price Range for Complete Sets in Good Condition: $75.00 to 125.00

Scenic Structures

Known Pattern Pieces: Tea set for four or six
Point of Origin, Date: Germany; circa 1890-1900
Colors, Ware Type, Features: Typical German set of blanks with decals of castles, wind mills and manor houses
Identical Blanks with Different Decorations: Not in exactness
Measurements: Teapot, 5¾"; sugar, 3½"; creamer, 3½"; cup, 2"; saucer, 4¼"
Classification: Scarce
Collection: Lundquest
Price Range for Complete Sets in Good Condition: $125.00 to 150.00

German Holly

Known Pattern Pieces: Tea set
Point of Origin, Date: Germany; 1890-1900
Colors, Ware Type, Features: Porcelain with light shades of red holly with green leaves ringing the rims
Identical Blanks with Different Decorations: Sets with children or flowers; see *Children's Glass Dishes, China and Furniture*, page 183
Measurements: Teapot, 5¾"; creamer, 3¼"; sugar, 3¾"; cup, 2"; saucer, 4½"; plate, 5¾"
Classification: Obtainable
Collection: Lechler
Price Range for Complete Sets in Good Condition: $150.00 to 250.00

Rose Bud

Known Pattern Pieces: Tea set
Point of Origin, Date: Germany; 1900's; Blue Meissen (type) mark on unglazed bottom
Colors, Ware Type, Features: White porcelain with cut and applied rose bud finials and hand painted roses; unusual pot with upright handle; footed creamer; open sugar
Measurements: Teapot with extended handle, 3¾" from top of handle to base; teapot, 2½"; open sugar, 1" tall; creamer 2"
Classification: Scarce
Collection: Lechler
Price Range for Complete Sets in Good Condition: $125.00 to 200.00
References or Author's Comments: See page 530 in *Marks on German, Bohemian and Austrian Porcelain 1710 to Present* by Rontgen.

Fuchsia Enameled

Known Pattern Pieces: Tea set
Point of Origin, Date: European
Colors, Ware Type, Features: White body with tin glaze fused to china; bright blues and soft blues; fine examples
Measurements: Teapot, 3¼"; sugar, 2½"; creamer, 2½"; cup, 2"; saucer, 3½"
Classification: Scarce
Collection: Schumaker
Price Range for Complete Sets in Good Condition: $150.00 to 175.00

Bent Bud

Known Pattern Pieces: Tea Set
Point of Origin, Date: European
Colors, Ware Type, Features: Porcelain with a tin glaze fused over the body; vivid accents of gold, chinese red and navy

Identical Blanks with Different Decorations: Plain white body with gold leaf-type designs
Measurements: Teapot, 3″; sugar, 2½″; creamer, 2″; cup, 1½″; saucer, 3″
Classification: Scarce
Collection: Baugh
Price Range for Complete Sets in Good Condition: $125.00 to 150.00

Measurements: Teapot, 3⅞″; sugar, 2″; creamer, 2⅜″; cup, 2″; saucer, 3¾″; tray 7⅞″ x 9½″
Classification: Obtainable
Collection: Hartzfeld
Price Range for Complete Sets in Good Condition: $75.00 to 125.00

Blue Elegance

Known Pattern Pieces: Tea set
Point of Origin, Date: Germany; 1900's
Colors, Ware Type, Features: White porcelain with blue design; footed main pieces; plates are the most difficult to locate; melon ribbing
Measurements: Teapot, 3½″; sugar, 3½″; creamer, 2½″; cup, 1½″; saucer, 4″; plate, about 6″ across
Classification: Common
Collection: Lechler
Price Range for Complete Sets in Good Condition: $50.00 to 100.00

Heavy Gold with Pink Roses

Known Pattern Pieces: Tea set
Point of Origin, Date: Germany; circa 1900's
Colors, Ware Type, Features: Porcelain with pink roses and heavy gold trim
Identical Blanks with Different Decorations: Found with other floral designs
Measurements: Teapot, 5½″; sugar, 3″; creamer, 3½″; cup, about 2″; saucer, 4½″; plate, 5″ across
Classification: Obtainable
Collection: Sembric
Price Range for Complete Sets in Good Condition: $75.00 to 125.00

Purple-Red Hearts with Stars

Known Pattern Pieces: Six-piece tea set
Point of Origin, Date: Germany; circa early 1900's
Colors, Ware Type, Features: Pearl skin on porcelain

Petite Christmas Holly

Known Pattern Pieces: Tea set
Point of Origin, Date: Germany; circa 1914
Colors, Ware Type, Features: Poorly made ware; interesting shape; Christmas holly decorations; long spout
Identical Blanks with Different Decorations: Various decorations, none well executed
Measurements: Teapot 4″ with spout being 2½″ long; sugar, 2″; creamer, 1¾″; cup, 1½″; saucer, 2½″
Classification: Obtainable

Collection: Lechler
Price Range for Complete sets in Good Condition: $125.00 to 150.00
References or Author's Comments: This set was sold by Marshall Field in 1914.

Peach Roses with Burnished Gold

Known Pattern Pieces: Tea set with chestnut or fruit bowls
Point of Origin, Date: Germany; 1914
Colors, Ware Type, Features: Porcelain with interesting shapes but poor decorations; dessert plates and fruit bowls appear with arcading
Identical Blanks with Different Decorations: Different floral or Christmas designs; also plain white with gold
Measurements: Teapot, around 5½"; sugar, 4"; creamer, 3"; cup, 1¾"; saucer, 3½"; pierced bowls, 4¾" across and 2" tall (2)
Classification: Obtainable
Collection: Baugh
Price Range for Complete sets in Good Condition: $75.00 to 165.00
References or Author's Comments: Arcading describes a type of pierced rim usually found on dessert ware or fruit baskets. These dishes were used to serve chestnuts or fruit.

Cobalt Berolina

Known Pattern Pieces: Tea set
Point of Origin, Date: Marked "Berolina"
Colors, Ware Type, Features: Cobalt over all with patches of white embellished with floral clusters

Identical Blanks with Different Decorations: May be found with various floral clusters; may be found in granite ware
Measurements: Teapot, 3½"; sugar, 2½"; creamer, 2", cup, 1¾"; saucer, 3½"
Classification: Obtainable in china
Collection: Private
Price Range for Complete sets in Good Condition: $45.00 to 65.00

Imari (style) Tete-A-Tete
(first set on left)

Known Pattern Pieces: Tray, teapot, sugar, creamer, two cups and saucers
Point of Origin, Date: England
Colors, Ware Type, Features: Cobalt, red, green and gold all over, except on bases--blue flows slightly
Measurements: Tray, 4" long; teapot, 2"; sugar, 1"; creamer, 1¼"; cup, ¾"; saucer, 1½"
Classification: Rare
Collection: Lechler
Price Range for Complete sets in Good Condition: $200.00 to 275.00
References or Author's Comments: Imari is named for a Japanese port called Imari. Porcelain was shipped from Imari. Imari (type) ware is pure white and hard. Early pieces were modeled after Chinese blue and white ware which had a great deal of Chinese red enamel. European factories copied this colorful ware, so the name "Imari" means any pattern of this style.

Silver and Orange on White
(set on right in photo above)

Known Pattern Pieces: Tray, 2 cups and saucers, teapot, sugar and creamer
Point of Origin, Date: Germany; 1900's
Colors, Ware Type, Features: Porcelain; melon ribbing on three main pieces; lavish silver trim; hand painted accents of orange
Measurements: Tray, 4¼"; teapot, 1½"; sugar, 1¼"; creamer, 1¼"; cup, ½"; saucer, 1¼"
Classification: Unusual with silver trim
Collection: Lechler
Price Range for Complete sets in Good Condition: $75.00 to 100.00

Butterflies and Flowers

Known Pattern Pieces: Beverage set for four
Point of Origin, Date: European
Colors, Ware Type, Features: Semi-porcelain with different flowers and butterflies decorating each piece
Classification: Obtainable
Collection: Lechler
Price Range for Complete sets in Good Condition: $75.00 to 100.00

GERMAN TEA SETS, CHILDREN, ANIMALS AND NURSERY TALES

*Christmas

Known Pattern Pieces: Tea set tor four or six
Point of Origin, Date: Germany; circa 1890-1900
Colors, Ware Type, Features: Porcelain with vivid scenes of Christmas
Identical Blanks with Different Decorations: Old Fashioned Girl and Dog; All Over Pink Luster; see *Children's Glass Dishes, China and Furniture*, page 183 and page 202
Measurements: Teapot, 5¼"; sugar, 3¼"; creamer, 3¼"; cup, 2"; saucer, 4½"; plate, 5¼"
Classification: Scarce
Collection: Private
Price Range for Complete Sets in Good Condition: $275.00 to 375.00

German Christmas

Known Pattern Pieces: Tea set for four or six
Point of Origin, Date: Germany; circa 1890-1900
Colors, Ware Type, Features: Porcelain with children playing ball; words "Merry Christmas"
Identical Blanks with Different Decorations: See exact plate on page 202 of *Children's Glass Dishes, China and Furniture*; also see, page 154, Lilac and Begonia
Measurements: Teapot, 5½"; sugar, 3¼"; creamer, 3½"; cup, 1¾"; saucer, 4⅛"; plate, 5¼"
Classification: Scarce in Christmas motif
Collection: Lundquest
Price Range for Complete Sets in Good Condition: $275.00 to 325.00

Sledding Home With Packages and Tree

Known Pattern Pieces: Tea set for four or six
Point of Origin, Date: Germany; circa 1880
Colors, Ware Type, Features: Porcelain with decals of Christmas preparations; boy on sled with a tree; girl on sled with two bundles

Identical Blanks with Different Decorations: Boy and Dog; Titled Nursery Rhymes; *Children's Glass Dishes, China and Furniture*, pages 168 and 169

Measurements: Teapot, 5″; sugar, 3″; creamer, 3½″; cup, 2⅜″; saucer, 4¼″; plate, 5″

Classification: Rare because of Christmas indication

Collection: Lundquest

Price Range for Complete Sets in Good Condition: $275.00 to 375.00

References or Author's Comments: Sets with Christmas indications sell for more money than other designs on identical blanks because it is a special collecting classification

Victorian Ladies

Angel and Star (Merry Christmas)

Known Pattern Pieces: Tea set for six

Point of Origin, Date: Germany; circa 1900

Colors, Ware Type, Features: Porcelain with poorly executed pictures; gold trim; angel standing in a meadow; tree, building in background; star; bridge; water; winter colors; Merry Christmas

Identical Blanks with Different Decorations: See *Children's Glass Dishes, China and Furniture*, page 174, Children on Sled; Kissing; Two Girls with Doll; Fairy Tale Variety

Measurements: Teapot, 6¼″; sugar, 4″; creamer, 4″; cup, 2¼″; saucer, 4½″; plate, 5¼″

Classification: Scarce because of Christmas motif

Collection: Lechler

Price Range for Complete Sets in Good Condition: $300.00 to 375.00

Known Pattern Pieces: Tea setting for six

Point of Origin, Date: Germany

Colors, Ware Type, Features: Decals of Victorian ladies on porcelain; gold trim

Identical Blanks with Different Decorations: Girl with a Whip; White Open Roses (see *Children's Glass Dishes, China and Furniture*, pages 177, 178)

Measurements: Teapot, 4¾″; sugar, 2⁷⁄₁₆″; creamer, 3″; cup, 1⅞″; saucer, 4⅛″; plate, 5¼″

Classification: Obtainable

Collection: Hartzfeld

Price Range for Complete Sets in Good Condition: $150.00 to 350.00

Snowman and Children

Known Pattern Pieces: Tea set for four or six
Point of Origin, Date: Germany; circa 1890-1900
Colors, Ware Type, Features: Porcelain with bright Christmas (type) decals; girls in a grand array of apparel showing that they are from families of "means"; snowman sports a carrot nose; teapot with split handle
Identical Blanks with Different Decorations: Busy Day; Clown's see *Children's Glass Dishes, China and Furniture*, page 171; see (also) this book, Dutch People
Measurements: Teapot, 5½"; sugar, 3½"; creamer, 3¼" cup, 2"; saucer, 4¼"; plate, 6"
Classification: Scarce
Collection: Lundquest
Price Range for Complete Sets in Good Condition: $200.00 to 350.00
References or Author's Comments: Children and winter scenes are higher in price than "like" blanks with more common decals.

Dutch People

Known Pattern Pieces: Tea set for six
Point of Origin, Date: Germany; circa 1890-1900
Colors, Ware Type, Features: Porcelain with vivid decals of Dutch people which also appear on English ware impressed "Newland", Stoke-On-Trent
Identical Blanks with Different Decorations: Clowns, See *Children's Glass Dishes, China and Furniture*, page 171; see (also) this book, Snowman and Children
Measurements: Teapot, 5½"; sugar, 3½"; creamer, 3¼"; cup, 2"; saucer, 4¼"; plate, 6"
Classification: Obtainable
Collection: Steffen
Price Range for Complete Sets in Good Condition: $150.00 to 175.00

Florence

Known Pattern Pieces: Tea set for six
Point of Origin, Date: Germany; circa 1890-1900
Colors, Ware Type, Features: Porcelain with pastels and gilt trim; girls are seen on comb and mirror sets and vases
Identical Blanks with Different Decorations: To Grandmother's House, pages 187 and 188 in *Children's Glass Dishes, China and Furniture*
Measurements: Teapot, 6⅛"; sugar, 3¾"; creamer, 4"; cup, 2¼"; saucer, 4¼"; plate, 5¼"
Classification: Scarce
Collection: Private
Price Range for Complete Sets in Good Condition: $125.00 to 200.00

The Cats' Thanksgiving

Known Pattern Pieces: Tea set for four or six
Point of Origin, Date: Germany
Colors, Ware Type, Features: Porcelain with gold trim and vivid, explicit details; Mother Cat holding the turkey with onlookers; at the table eating and after dinner rocking
Identical Blanks with Different Decorations: See *Children's Glass Dishes, China and Furniture*, page 182 and 183; plain blank and (also) Merry Christmas Angel
Measurements: Teapot, 5⅞"; sugar, 2⅜"; cup, 2⅜"; saucer, 4⅝"; plate, 6"
Classification: Scarce
Collection: Freshour
Price Range for Complete Sets in Good Condition: $275.00 to 325.00

Clown and Animals on Pigs

Known Pattern Pieces: Tea setting for six
Point of Origin, Date: Germany; circa 1890-1900
Colors, Ware Type, Features: Bright decals on white ware; luster trim; decals available on different blanks
Identical Blanks with Different Decorations: Merry Christmas in gold with pink or green accent trim
Measurements: Teapot, 4¾" sugar, 3½"; creamer, 3"; cup, 2"; saucer, 4½"; plate, 6"
Classification: Obtainable
Collection: Lundquest
Price Range for Complete Sets in Good Condition: $150.00 to 175.00
References or Author's Comments: The "Merry Christmas" motif on this same set of blanks would sell for quite a bit more because of the specialized collectors.

German Circus With Steiff Animals and Clowns

Known Pattern Pieces: Tea or coffee set for six
Point of Origin, Date: Germany
Colors, Ware Type, Features: Colorful decals of circus activities
Identical Blanks with Different Decorations: Old Fashion Girl and Dog; Gold Trimmed Pink Luster (see *Children's Glass Dishes, China and Furniture*, page 183)
Measurements: Teapot, 5¾"; sugar, 3¾"; creamer, 3¼"; cup, 2"; saucer, 4½"; plate, 5¾"

Classification: Obtainable
Collection: Hartzfeld
Price Range for Complete Sets in Good Condition: $100.00 to 125.00
References or Author's Comments: Steiff "Quaggy Duck" (left) has mohair head and arms. Its feet are natural rubber which tends to deteriorate. A mint duck costs about $95.00, but one in poor condition sells for only $70.00. The duck has a jointed head. The two clowns, 5½″ and 8½″, are called "Clownie" and were made in the early 1950's. The jointed 5½″ clown sells for $65.00 and the 8½″ clown sells for $85.00.

The Steiff chicken is a dressed "Kiki" and is 5″ tall with mohair arms and head. Its feet are rubber and the head is jointed. "Kiki" sells for $95.00 to 125.00, depending on condition. The velvet boar in this picture is 3″ tall. It is a wild baby boar with spots, felt ears, nose and tongue. Its tail has been wax dipped for curling purposes. The boar sells for $35.00. It is a Steiff product.

Children's Frolic

Known Pattern Pieces: Tea or coffee set for six
Point of Origin, Date: Germany; Franz Prause Porcelain Factory; 1894-1936
Colors, Ware Type, Features: Porcelain; slat-sided moulding; vivid, detailed decals of children playing "Blind Man's Bluff, "See-Saw Margery Daw" and "Circle Freeze"
Identical Blanks with Different Decorations: See *Children's Glass Dishes, China and Furniture*, pages 175, 176; Girl with Bears; Yellow Roses with Purple Luster; Pink and White Leaved Caladium
Measurements: Teapot, 6″; sugar, 4″; creamer, 3½″; cup, 2⅛″; saucer, 4½″; plate, 5″
Classification: Obtainable
Collection: Lundquest
Price Range for Complete Sets in Good Condition: Children's Frolic, $250.00 to 275.00, Girls With Bears: $375.00 to 400.00
References or Author's Comments: Any item with bears has a market today. The china sets with bears cost more than those with children or flowers, even if they appear on identical blanks.

Rain Storm

Known Pattern Pieces: Tea set for four or six
Point of Origin, Date: Germany; late 1800's to 1914
Colors, Ware Type, Features: Porcelain with colorful decals and interesting scenes of childhood--children with umbrella, cat and yarn, children on see-saw, children musicians, dog, butterfly, dish
Identical Blanks with Different Decorations: Identical decals found on page 137 and 178 of *Children's Glass Dishes, China and Furniture*
Measurements: Teapot, 5½″; sugar, 4″; creamer, 3¼″; cup, 1¾″; saucer, 4¼″
Classification: Scarce
Collection: Lundquest
Price Range for Complete Sets in Good Condition: $175.00 to 225.00

RS Portrait Scenes

Known Pattern Pieces: Tea set
Point of Origin, Date: Germany; 1898-1900
Colors, Ware Type, Features: Court-type portrait series featuring ladies and gentlemen; bunchy sugar bowl without handles; sugar and teapot have same lid; melon-moulded blanks sprinkled with gold leaves; soft aqua coloring
Measurements: Teapot, 4″; sugar, creamer and cups are 2″ tall; saucer, 4″
Classification: Rare
Collection: Lechler
Price Range for Complete Sets in Good Condition: $350.00 to 400.00
References or Author's Comments: None of the RS products in this book are marked. A toy set which is marked is shown in *Children's Glass Dishes, China and Furniture* on page 159. "Baby Red Roses With Gold Draping".

Identical Blanks with Different Decorations: Two styles of toy ware were sold and are shown in this publication. The list of subjects shown on these two blanks are as follows: Fruit (setting for six); Mother Goose or Bayreuth Nursery Jingles; Sand Babies; Billowy Girl; Sledding Babies; Boy with Geese and Donkey; Playing Children; Children's Scenes; Plain White with Gold Bands; Plump Boy and Girl (with horn and buggy)
Measurements: Tea kettle (style) handle (set); teapot, 5″ tall; sugar, 3½″; creamer, 2¼″; cup, 2¼″; saucer, 4½″, small tea ware size: teapot, 4″; sugar, 3½″; creamer, 2½″; cup, 2″; saucer, 4¼″
Classification: Scarce in completion
Collection: Lechler
Price Range for Complete Sets in Good Condition: $375.00 to 500.00
References or Author's Comments: Royal Bayreuth porcelain works was founded in Tettau, Bavaria in 1794. It continues as a subsidiary of Royal Tettau. (The products produced are dinnerware items and limited editions) Marks, when placed at all, were applied with decals or rubber stamps. Many versions of the Royal Bayreuth mark are known, but few were applied to toy ware.

Sunbonnet Babies

Royal Bayreuth Scenes (two tea shapes)

Known Pattern Pieces: Tea sets for two to six
Point of Origin, Date: Germany; circa 1900-1914; sold by Marshall Field and Company in 1914
Colors, Ware Type, Features: Porcelain with all over decoration; tea kettle (type) teapot difficult to locate; sets were sold in 9, 11,12 or 23 pieces to the box in 1914

Known Pattern Pieces: European tea set
Point of Origin, Date: European; circa 1890-1920
Colors, Ware Type, Features: Vivid all-over color; lavish gold trim; Sunbonnet girls are doing their weekly, never ending, chores
Classification: Rare
Collection: Strong Museum, card catalogue numbers 74.777, 74.784, 74.766, 74.861, 74.765, 74.850

Price Range for Complete Sets in Good Condition: $500.00 to 700.00

References or author's comments: Molly and May were created by Bertha L. Corbett Melchner. Without seeing the faces of these two Sunbonnet girls, they are known, loved and collected. *The Sunbonnet Babies* was written by Eulalie Osgood and lavishly illustrated by Bertha Melchner. The book was published in 1902 with the faceless girls becoming more famous than either the author or illustrator.

Housekeeping

Known Pattern Pieces: Tea set for four or six
Point of Origin, Date: Germany; circa 1890-1914
Colors, Ware Type, Features: Quality porcelain with vivid decals of store keepers; housekeepers and tea-time drinkers; green luster
Measurements: Teapot: 3″; sugar, 2″; creamer, 1¾″; cup, 2½″; saucer, 4″; plate, 5″
Classification: Scarce
Collection: Sembric
Price Range for Complete Sets in Good Condition: $200.00 to 250.00

White on White Animals

Known Pattern Pieces: Tea set
Point of Origin, Date: European
Colors, Ware Type, Features: White quality porcelain with an animal in relief on each side of the pieces
Classification: Scarce
Collection: Sembric
Price Range for Complete Sets in Good Condition: $100.00 to 175.00

Circus Tricks

Known Pattern Pieces: Tea set for four or six
Point of Origin, Date: Germany
Colors, Ware Type, Features: Luster on porcelain; vivid decals of animals; clown on a mule; monkey pulling a wheelbarrow; clown on a ball
Identical Blanks with Different Decorations: Busy Girl, pages 171 and 172 of *Children's Glass Dishes, China and Furniture*
Measurements: Teapot, 4⅜″; creamer, 3″; sugar, 3¼″; cup, 2″; saucer, 4¼″; plate, 5″
Classification: Obtainable
Collection: Lechler
Price Range for Complete Sets in Good Condition: $150.00 to 175.00

Cat Band

Known Pattern Pieces: Tea set or four or six
Point of Origin, Date: Germany
Colors, Ware Type, Features: Gold luster on very white (quality) porcelain; colorful, vivid decals with other luster colored accents; cats reading and playing instruments
Measurements: Teapot, 5"; plate, 6"; saucer, 4½"
Classification: Obtainable
Collection: Lechler
Price Range for Complete Sets in Good Condition: $100.00 to 175.00

At The Circus

Known Pattern Pieces: Tea for two; original box
Point of Origin, Date: Germany
Colors, Ware Type, Features: Thin porcelain with gold and gray luster; vivid decals of elephants, donkeys and dogs
Identical Blanks with Different Decorations: Sunbonnet Girls; Alice In Wonderland, page 189 and 190 in *Children's Glass Dishes, China and Furniture*
Measurements: Teapot, 3¾"; sugar, (open) 1¾"; creamer, 3"; cup, 1¾"; saucer, 4"; plate, 5"
Classification: Obtainable
Collection: Lechler
Price Range for Complete Sets in Good Condition: $60.00 to 150.00 depending on decals
References or Author's Comments: The set of Sunbonnet Girls on this blank was not very well executed, so the price, which would ordinarily be high, is reduced. Condition plays a great part in pricing toy ware.

Fun-loving Children also Tease A Kitten

Known Pattern Pieces: Tea or coffee for six
Point of Origin, Date: Germany; circa 1900-1937
Colors, Ware Type, Features: Excellent porcelain with outstandingly vivid decals of children in outfits which look like the ones worn by the street people in "My Fair Lady"
Identical Blanks with Different Decorations: Tease a Kitten shown in this publication; other sets with chidlren's scenes
Measurements: Teapot, 6"; sugar, 3½"; creamer, 2⅝"; cup, 2"; saucer, 4⅜"; plate, 5¼"

Classification: Obtainable
Collection: Lechler
Price Range for Complete Sets in Good Condition: $100.00 to 200.00

Driving Animals

Known Pattern Pieces: Tea or coffee set
Point of Origin, Date: European; turn of the century
Colors, Ware Type, Features: Porcelain with gold trim and animal decals; animals are driving cars and motorcycles
Measurements: (Approximate measurements) teapot, 5¼"; sugar, 3¼"; creamer, 2¾"; cup, 1¾"; saucer, 4¼"
Classification: Obtainable
Collection: Strong Museum, card catalogue number 82.407
Price Range for Complete Sets in Good Condition: $100.00 to 125.00

Cupid

Known Pattern Pieces: Tea set
Point of Origin, Date: European; turn of the century
Colors, Ware Type, Features: Elegant handles; fine lines on porcelain gold accents on pale blue; white cupid in slight relief
Classification: Obtainable
Collection: Freshour
Price Range for Complete Sets in Good Condition: $125.00 to 175.00

Ethnic Group

Known Pattern Pieces: Tea set
Point of Origin, Date: European
Colors, Ware Type, Features: Except for the saucers, each piece of this set features an Indian face
Classification: Scarce
Collection: Hartzfeld
Price Range for Complete Sets in Good Condition: $300.00 to 450.00

Indians

Known Pattern Pieces: Tea set
Point of Origin, Date: European; turn of the century
Colors, Ware Type, Features: Porcelain; decalcomania; decorated with four different pictures of famous Indians; titled: Sitting Bull, Spotted Horse etc.
Identical Blanks with Different Decorations: Similar to Romantic in this book and Robinson Crusoe in *Children's Glass Dishes, China and Furniture*, page 184
Measurements: Teapot, 4⅜"; sugar, 2"; creamer, 3"; cup, 2"; saucer, 3¼"; cake server, 4¼"
Classification: Obtainable
Collection: Strong Museum, card catalogue number 77.3046
Price Range for Complete Sets in Good Condition: $100.00 to 150.00

Romantic

Known Pattern Pieces: Tea set for two with cake servers
Point of Origin, Date: European; turn of the century
Colors, Ware Type, Features: Decals of romantic scenes on stark white ware
Identical Blanks with Different Decorations: Similar to Robinson Crusoe on page 184 of *Children's Glass Dishes, China and Furniture*; similar to Ethnic Group in this book
Measurements: Teapot, 4⅜"; sugar, 2"; creamer, 3"; cup, 2"; saucer, 3¼"; cake plate, 4½"
Classification: Obtainable
Collection: Sembric
Price Range for Complete Sets in Good Condition: $50.00 to 100.00

GERMAN DINNER AND HOUSEKEEPING SETS

FELDBLUMEN (correct name)

Known Pattern Pieces: Dinner set
Point of Origin, Date: Germany; Villeroy & Boch, Wallerfangen; circa 1870
Colors, Ware Type, Features: Two sizes in dinner ware; large enough to have been used in the nursery; greenish-blue flowers
Identical Blanks with Different Decorations: Two dinner ware sizes; may have been sold with Different Decorations
Measurements: Soup bowl, 6" across; open compote, 2¼" tall and 6¼" across; gravy with underplate, 4"; serving platters: 7", 8", 8½" long; covered compote, 7" tall; (2) covered dishes, 4" tall; plates, 6". Smaller set: covered tureen, 5"; chop plate, 6"; (2) platters: 5", 6¼"; open compote, 1¾" tall; soups and plates, 4¼" across
Classification: Obtainable
Collection: Lechler
Price Range for Complete Sets in Good Condition: $200.00 to 300.00

Oyster Stew Set

Known Pattern Pieces: 18 Pieces in original box
Point of Origin, Date: Germany
Colors, Ware Type, Features: China with granite look; all over white with blue spray decoration; gold trim
Identical Blanks with Different Decorations: Same set of blanks with other color decorations
Measurements: Stew pot, 3¼"; plate, 3½"; soup bowls, 3" across and ½" deep; sauce boat with attached under plate, 1¼" tall and 2¾" across plate length; salad (square) dish, 1" tall and 2½" across; round server, ¾" tall and 3" across; oval plate, 4½" long; round ruffled plate, 3½" across

Classification: Scarce
Collection: Lechler
Price Range for Complete Sets in Good Condition: $225.00 to 325.00

Elegant Pink Roses

Known Pattern Pieces: Dinner set
Point of Origin, Date: Germany; circa 1880
Colors, Ware Type, Features: Fine ware with pink flowers and gold trim
Identical Blanks with Different Decorations: Other floral decorations
Measurements: Plate, 3½″; open compote, 2½″; covered serving dish, 2½″; oval platter, 5¼″; covered server, 4″; sauce with attached plate 2″ tall and 3½″ long
Classification: Obtainable
Collection: Lechler
Price Range for Complete Sets in Good Condition: $175.00 to 200.00
References or Author's Comments: There is a tea set with very similar decoration and body style

Chowder Set

Known Pattern Pieces: Housekeeping set
Point of Origin, Date: Germany; also Japan; circa 1914; this set is marked "Germany", red mark with 60 in center of circle
Colors, Ware Type, Features: Porcelain with peaches or flowers
Identical Blanks with Different Decorations: Sets sold with various flower or fruit designs
Measurements: Tureens: 3″ tall and 5″ long (2); (1) 3″ tall and 3½″ long; sauce attached plate 4½″ long and 1⅞″ tall; plate, 5″
Classification: Obtainable

Collection: Private
Price Range for Complete Sets in Good Condition: $200.00 to 225.00
References or Author's Comments: These sets are shown in the 1914 Marshall Field & Company, Kringle Society catalogue, Hobby Press

Red Roses

Known Pattern Pieces: Large dinner set in juvenile size
Point of Origin, Date: Unmarked; European
Colors, Ware Type, Features: Quality porcelain with chains of greenery and roses; gold accents
Classification: Difficult to find in completion
Collection: Private
Price Range for Complete Sets in Good Condition: $200.00 to 300.00

FRENCH TEA SETS

*Paris Scenic

Known Pattern Pieces: Tea set for four
Point of Origin, Date: France; 1890-1910
Colors, Ware Type, Features: Porcelain with lush hand painting; house with smoke from chimney; lavender floral designs around the house; peach colored road with black accents
Identical Blanks with Different Decorations: Brown-maroon flowers--see *Children's Glass Dishes, China and Furniture*, page 146; other floral sets known

Measurements: Teapot, 5″; sugar, 3″; creamer, 2¾″; cup, 1½″; deep saucer, 2½″ across; plate, 3″
Classification: Scarce
Collection: Lechler
Price Range for Complete Sets in Good Condition: $125.00 to 175.00
References or Author's Comments: This set seems to measure slightly larger than the brown-maroon flowers shown in *Children's Glass Dishes, China and Furniture*

Gothic

Known Pattern Pieces: Tea set for two
Point of Origin, Date France
Colors, Ware Type, Features: Hand painted decoration; many colored scenes of landscape and buildings
Identical Blanks with Different Decorations: See *Children's Glass Dishes, China and Furniture*, page 161, "Pink Rose Buds" with tray; see (also) this publication, set in original basket
Measurements: Teapot, 3″ tall; sugar, 3″; creamer, 2½″; cup, 1″; saucer, 2¾″; square tray (not with Gothic set), 5½″ x 5½″
Classification: Obtainable
Collection: Strong Museum, card catalogue number 77.3015
Price Range for Complete Sets in Good Condition: Gothic, $125.00 to 145.00

Soft Blue with Gold

Known Pattern Pieces: Tea set for four
Point of Origin, Date European
Colors, Ware Type, Features: Footed main pieces; over all exterior, soft blue accented by gold; porcelain; ornate handles
Identical Blanks with Different Decorations: Floral designs
Measurements: Teapot, 3½″; creamer, 2½″; cup, 1⅛″; saucer, 2½″
Classification: Obtainable
Collection: Private
Price Range for Complete Sets in Good Condition: $45.00 to 75.00

*French Packaging

Known Pattern Pieces: Tea set for six plus spoons and basket
Point of Origin, Date France; circa 1903
Colors, Ware Type, Features: Porcelain with hand painted blue berries, green leaves and gold trim; there is no creamer and no sugar in this packaged basket
Identical Blanks with Different Decorations: See Gothic in this publication and "Pink Rose Buds" in *Children's Glass Dishes, China and Furniture*, page 161
Measurements: Teapot, 2″; no sugar, no creamer; cup, 1″; saucer, 2″; spoons, 2½″; basket (not counting handle), 7¼″; total basket height, 14″
Classification: Very rare as packaged
Collection: Lechler
Price Range for Complete Sets in Good Condition: $500.00 to 600.00

References or Author's Comments: A set found in this condition with all original parts including the string holding the package together is very unusual. Since France could not compete with the German market, the stores often packaged German products and sold them as their own. The basket, in this case, is marked France.

French Coffee or Tea Set

Known Pattern Pieces: Coffee set for four
Point of Origin, Date France
Colors, Ware Type, Features: Coffee pot is a tea or coffee vessel. It has two strainer sections, a tea pot and a lid; the set is chocolate in color with high glaze; handles on tall strainer section; white interior
Measurements: Teapot base, 2″, tall strainer section, 2¼″, small strainer, ½″, total height, 5″; sugar, 2½″; cup, 1½″; saucer, 3¼″
Classification: Rare
Collection: Lechler
Price Range for Complete Sets in Good Condition: $150.00 to 225.00

French Floral

Known Pattern Pieces: Tea set
Point of Origin, Date France; circa 1890-1900; marked "S.B.V. et V ie France"
Colors, Ware Type, Features: Porcelain with tiny floral clusters with red and light blue accent trim; unusual toy shape
Measurements: Teapot, 4¼″; creamer, 2″; saucer, 3¾″

Classification: Uncommon
Collection: Lechler
Price Range for Complete Sets in Good Condition: $125.00 to 175.00

Bonne Nuit (night maid)

Known Pattern Pieces: Three-part unit for tea (veilleuse)
Point of Origin, Date: France; Limoges; 20th century; base decal of woman musician playing mandolin and man dancing
Colors, Ware Type, Features: Flowers on porcelain; a chamberstick and candle furnish the heat with the candle available when needed for guidance; decalcomania; brass lid (may not be original)
Measurements: Child-size, used by adults as well; functional
Classification: Unusual
Collection: Strong Museum, card catalogue number 77.3025
Price Range for Complete Sets in Good Condition: $100.00 to 175.00

94

French Boys and Girls

Known Pattern Pieces: Tea or coffee set for four or six
Point of Origin, Date: France; circa 1900-1937; marked "MODELE u-f France Depose"
Colors, Ware Type, Features: Decals of children on porcelain
Measurements: Teapot, 5¼″; sugar, 3¼″; creamer, 2¾″; cup, 1¾″; saucer, 4½″
Classification: Obtainable
Collection: Lundquest
Price Range for Complete Sets in Good Condition: $125.00 to 150.00

Violets on Soft Paste

Known Pattern Pieces: Tea set for four
Point of Origin, Date: European
Colors, Ware Type, Features: Grayish soft paste body with interesting lines and hand painted flowers

Identical Blanks with Different Decorations: Similar blank shown here with Different Decorations; obviously from the same company
Measurements: Violets on Soft Paste: teapot, 5½″; sugar, 3¼″; creamer, 3¼″; cup, 2″; saucer, 3¼″
Classification: Obtainable
Collection: Sembric; Hamilton
Price Range for Complete Sets in Good Condition: $50.00 to 100.00

FRENCH DINNER SETS

*French Children

Known Pattern Pieces: Large dinner set for twelve
Point of Origin, Date: France; marked "Luneville K. & G." encircled in a belt-like design; another mark on the set is a cloud burst over an X with the word "FRANCE"
Colors, Ware Type, Features: Rose on white earthenware; many different scenes of children: child on a dog, flying birds, girl in a goat cart, dancing couple, boy and goat, woman and child with animal, boy with cow and boy and goat; boy and drum
Measurements: Double dip dish, 2¼″ long; round, open vegetable, 2¾″; open compote, 2″ tall and 3½″ across; covered tureen with attached plate, 1¾″ tall; covered tureen with plate, 3½″; covered dishes: 3″, 4½″; large open bowl, 2″ tall and 4½″ across; platters: (2) 4¼″, 5¼″, (2) 6¼″ (platters are fish-shaped); plates: 4″, 4½″; soup, 4″; (2) open compotes, 2¼″ tall and 3¾″ across
Classification: Rare
Collection: Lechler
Price Range for Complete Sets in Good Condition: $425.00 to 600.00

French Stencils

Known Pattern Pieces: Tea and dinner ware
Point of Origin, Date: France; circa 1890-1920
Colors, Ware Type, Features: Red and green stencils on French soft paste
Measurements: Covered dishes: 5″, 3¾″; serving bowls; platter, 4½″ x 6½″; plates: 5½″, 4¾″; cup, 2″; saucers, 3¼″
Classification: Scarce
Collection: Steffen
Price Range for Complete Sets in Good Condition: $200.00 to 300.00

French-In-The Box

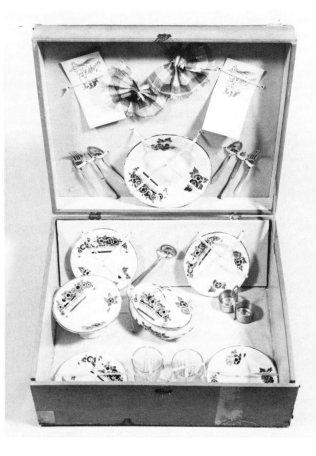

Known Pattern Pieces: Dinner china, two glass tumblers, metal flatware and serving pieces, napkins
Point of Origin, Date: Paris, France; circa 1900-1914
Colors, Ware Type, Features: Orange, blue and green floral designs on porcelain
Measurements: 12″ across box, 10″ deep, 5″ high; tureen, 2½″ tall and 4½″ across; compote, 2″ tall, 3½″across; soup, 3⅝″ across; plate, 3⅝″ across; round server, 4½″ across; tumbler, 1¾″ tall
Classification: Rare in completion
Collection: Lechler
Price Range for Complete Sets in Good Condition: $175.00 to 275.00

Forget-Me-Nots and Pink Trim

Known Pattern Pieces: Dinner set
Point of Origin, Date: European
Colors, Ware Type, Features: Lavender and pink bands around a forget-me-not design; gold trim
Measurements: (2) Open footed dishes, 1½″ tall and 2¾″ across; (2) matching oval platters, 4″ long and 2½″ across; covered deep dish, 2½″ tall; sauce boat, 1¾″ tall and 3″ long; a double dip dish, 2¾″ long; compote cake-type server, 3¾″ tall; deep vegetable bowl, 2″ tall and 3½″ wide; tureen, 3½″; soup bowls, 3″ across; plate, 3″ across
Classification: Scarce
Collection: Lechler
Price Range for Complete Sets in Good Condition: $200.00 to 275.00

AMERICAN TEA AND DINNER SETS
Blue Spongeware

Known Pattern Pieces: Tea set for six
Point of Origin, Date: America; Burford Bros., East Liverpool, Ohio; circa 1879-1905
Colors, Ware Type, Features: Sponge spotted ware with design seeping through; ironstone; root beer barrel-shaped finials
Identical blanks with different decorations: Old Moss Rose
Measurements: Teapot, 5¼″; sugar, 4¾″; creamer, 3¾″; plate, 4¾″; cup, 2¼″; saucer, 4½″
Classification: Rare

Collection: Lechler
Price Range for Complete Sets in Good Condition: $375.00 to 500.00
References or Author's Comments: Sponging ware for decoration was a fast, cheap form of decorating cottage pottery which was developed in Scottish potteries. A sponge dipped into color left its stamp on the ware, often seeping into the interior of the pottery. This ware filtered down to the working class.

Ironstone with Flowers

Known Pattern Pieces: Tea set
Point of Origin, Date: American
Colors, Ware Type, Features: Ironstone with blue flowers; solid
Identical Blanks with Different Decorations: Other floral and nursery rhyme designs; plain with gold bands
Measurements: Teapot, 5¼″; sugar, 4½″; creamer, 3¼″; cup, 2¼″; saucers, 4½″; plates, 6¼″
Classification: Obtainable
Collection: Lundquest
Price Range for Complete Sets in Good Condition: $50.00 to 75.00

Robin Red Breast (correct name)

Known Pattern Pieces: Six-place setting for tea
Point of Origin, Date: America; George Scott Pottery, Cincinnati, Ohio; two different Scott marks on this set; even one Scott mark is difficult to locate
Colors, Ware Type, Features: Semi-porcelain with large and vivid displays of robins and branches
Measurements: Teapot, 5¼″; sugar, 5½″; creamer, 3¼″; cup, 2½″; saucer, 5¼″; plate, 4¾″

Classification: Rare
Collection: Lechler
Price Range for Complete Sets in Good Condition: $225.00 to 275.00
References or Author's Comments: The George Scott establishment was one of the largest of its kind in the country.

Rocky

Known Pattern Pieces: Tea set; functional dinner sets
Point of Origin, Date: America; Edwin M. Knowles
Colors, Ware Type, Features: Colorful decals on opaque china
Measurements: Teapot, 3¼″; sugar, 2¼″; creamer, 2½″; cup, 2¼″; saucer, 5¼″; plate, 6¼″
Classification: Obtainable
Collection: Rogers
Price Range for Complete Sets in Good Condition: $75.00 to 125.00

References or Author's Comments: The character "Rocky" was used on children's railroad china. "Rocky" is a prized pattern among collectors of railroad items. Some sets were made for the Great Northern dining cars in the 1920's and 1930's. Syracuse produced much of the dining car ware for children

Cinderella and the Prince

Known Pattern Pieces: Large, child-size tea set for six
Point of Origin, Date: America: Knowles, Taylor and Knowles; circa 1905-1929; marked "K.T. & K. s--v CHINA P.B.A."
Colors, Ware Type, Features: Earthenware; white body with pastel decals carrying the entire story line of Cinderella
Measurements: Teapot, 5¼″ wide and 2½″ tall; sugar, 4″ wide, 2″ tall; creamer, 2″ tall; cup, 2″; saucer, 5″; plate, 7″; waste bowl, 3½″ wide and 2¼″ tall
Classification: Difficult to complete with entire story
Collection: Sembric
Price Range for Complete Sets in Good Condition: $175.00 to 250.00

KATE GREENAWAY

Kate Greenaway, the plump enchantress who preferred little girls and boys who live in that "nice land" . . . the ones who come when called, fair or dark, in green ribbons or blue, acknowledged that she lived in a dream world. She spent her fifty-five years making cowslip fields grown and fruit trees bloom by a stroke of imagination. This shy, quiet little woman with dark, expressive eyes dealt with fame the same way she dealt with everyday life, with good humor and charm. She was too modest to realize the accolades heaped on her by two hemispheres.

After a study of two different works based on the life of Kate Greenaway, it's been deduced that the truth about her must be as elusive and mystical as her art work. *Kate Greenaway* by M.H. Spielmann and G.S. Layard and the book *KATE GREENAWAY* by Rodney Engen emphasize this view by comparison.

As in any other life in this world, hers was a cartwheel existence . . . that of being on top of the wheel in some instances and down in the mire in others. Kate nearly always was in a state of needing more money. Her father was a wood engraver and failed in the business world. Her mother, on the other hand, had a good head for business and the talent to carry a wealthy clientele in the millinery business. The clothing she designed for little girls must also have influenced Kate in later life to dress her paper family in proper style.

Kate was an introspective, shy child with emotional highs and lows and, of course, she was an acknowledged dreamer. As a child her expectations exceeded reality and when this happened, as it often will, she became depressed.

Kate grew up in several households, all in the city neighborhoods with other "crafts" people. When she could, Kate escaped to the garden to hide from the drab and the mundane.

She began a doll collection as a child and added to it throughout her life. Other interests included summers spent on a farm in Rolleston. This environment, which she loved best of all, was the source of many illustrations in later life. These illustrations were not true to life in many cases because Kate chose to escape disaster by painting it prettily. For instance, a terrible flood was romanticized in her book *Under The Window* with boys floating in tubs, seemingly having the time of their lives. This unrealistic view of the hardships of rural life in the nineteenth century was a form of withdrawal from unpleasantness and squalor. It was the country she loved, however, and when she had to leave it for town-life she became very difficult.

Kate attended several schools unsuccessfully and when there was a show of strain, Kate became mysteriously ill. She soon recovered, however, after her mother removed her from the offending situation. She studied at South Kensington and the London Slade School, with water color being the medium of greatest success for this gentle, bespectacled woman.

In 1868, her work made its first public showing with children appearing from a previous century. She painted them in their proper environment, away from the work-a-world in a place of total pleasantness.

As with many artists, her first saleable efforts produced very little in the way of profit, even though twenty-five thousand copies of her valentine sold in just a few weeks.

The Greenaway influence was evident in English attire around 1879. The examples of her designs were worn by the children creating a vogue which spread across the sea forging still another kinship with America.

Kate Greenaway's book, *Under the Window* published in 1878, holds some scenes which are sometimes found on sets of children's glass and china. Since each country wishes to claim Kate, they shared her by imparting her designs, verses and styles on countless products of the time. Her prim, neat children marched across magazines, almanacs and books, slipping into the collectors' lives by way of paper, glass, china, furniture, fabric, metal and buttons.

What did Kate Greenaway do to earn and gain such fame? She illustrated cards and a score or so of books and she produced some lovely and delicate water colors. Why then did she have a hold on two hemispheres? Why did each country strive to claim her? Why is her work still in demand and still copied today?

Some people born in this world have a special power to fascinate and attract--Kate Greenaway had this charisma. She attracted one special rascal, Mr. John Ruskin, in 1880. He was to bully, rule and influence her emotional and artistic world for nearly twenty years. Mr. Ruskin did not love Kate Greenaway. No indeed! He preferred little girls, falling in love with a ten year old child when he himself was forty. Kate, however, loved and admired Mr. Ruskin. When she was thirty seven she met the sixty-three year old Ruskin for the first time, other than by letter. She was dazzled by this difficult and demanding man who tried (unsuccessfully) on several occasions to persuade Kate to defrock her paper "Girlies".

Not only was Ruskin less than practical, telling Kate it was degradation to paint for money, he also encouraged her to change mediums and styles until her work not only suffered but was rejected by the public.

In 1885, Kate moved to her house in Hampstead, a move which infuriated Ruskin. Kate was secretly working on *Marigold Garden* because she knew that piece would not please him either. This particular publication shows the strain Kate was under with its inconsistent styles and confused verse. (It may have been, too, that like the equally famous Beatrix Potter, Kate Greenaway was simply a better artist than a writer.) Nonetheless, Kate's popularity faded in her home country of England, at that time. She was supported by the ever popular and generous American dollar.

The year 1891 was a time of personal and professional crises for Kate Greenaway with the largest show of her work (during her lifetime) bringing in less than the sales of her first book. Her landscapes were especially shunned.

In 1895, Kate visited Ruskin for the last time. He was so ill and delirious that Kate was able to communicate only in baby talk to the man who had the greatest influence on her life. She left his home embarrassed by her own inadequacies . . . once again.

During the winter of 1896, Kate's own health failed. Her thinking and creative abilities were much diminished. She was also a very lonely woman during this, the blackest period of her life.

On January 20, 1900, Ruskin died leaving Kate bereft. In July of that same year, Kate was operated on and it was found that cancer had spread throughout her chest.

On November 12, in the rain and wind, her flower-covered coffin was taken by road to Woking where she was cremated--an unusual practice for the time. The funeral was studiously simple and private. Kate's grave remains neglected and is obscured by the blossoming fruit trees which offered escape and protection in life as in death. The headstone inscribed with her own unpretentious and, in this case inadequate verse reads: "Heaven's blue skies may shine above my head,

While you stand there--

And say that I am dead."

A mysterious and permanent charm has encased all with which she was associated right down to the buttons on a frock. If an article has the Greenaway influence, it is a sure "seller" today.

The wispy-willowy-wistful figures found on the toy tea and dinner sets in this book enhance the already interesting shape and variety of these serviceable American pieces. The clean little girls found on the china emphasize the manners needed when serving one's little friends at a playhouse dinner. Who, indeed dared to create riot when one glance at the dinner ware showed the proper behavior to be emulated.

Note: Special thanks to Elaine Challacombe of the Margaret Woodbury Strong Museum Library in Rochester, New York for the information she provided concerning Kate Greenaway.

Kate Greenaway Illustrations

Known Pattern Pieces: Tea set for six
Point of Origin, Date: America; Vodrey Pottery Company, East Liverpool, Ohio; after 1879
Colors, Ware Type, Features: Gilding, pastels and repeated Greenaway motif; crazing
Identical Blanks with Different Decorations: Same blank with brown monochrome floral motif; also blue and green floral design on same white semi-porcelain body
Measurements: Teapot, 4¾"; plate, 4¾"; saucer, 4¾"
Classification: Common
Collection: Strong Museum, card catalogue number 76.4547
Price Range for Complete Sets in Good Condition: $135.00 to $175.00 Greenaway, $50.00 to 65.00 floral
References or Author's Comments: There are Kate Greenaway collectors who buy these tea sets. This motif would bring higher prices in general than the floral designs.

American Greenaway; Children and Dachshund

Known Pattern Pieces: Juvenile-size tea sets
Point of Origin, Date: America; circa 1900's
Colors, Ware Type, Features: Greenaway set has gilding and decals of children modeled after the style of Kate Greenaway's illustrations; the Children and Dachshund sets have an impish dog pulling the table cloth to the floor.
Identical Blanks with Different Decorations: Two different designs are presented here
Measurements: Teapot, 4½"; sugar, 4"; creamer, 3¾"; cup, 2" tall and 2¼" wide; saucer, 4¾"; plate, 7"; waste bowl, 2¾"
Classification: Obtainable
Collection: Kate Greenaway, Strong Museum; Children and Dachshund, Lundquest
Price Range for Complete Sets in Good Condition: $125.00 to 150.00
References or Author's Comments: Strong Museum card catalogue number 76.4542

Greenaway Dinner Set

Kate Greenaway (two different shapes and two different companies)

Known Pattern Pieces: Large dinner set
Point of Origin, Date: America; Knowles, Taylor and Knowles; 1870-1929
Colors, Ware Type, Features: Spring-colored decals; very detailed and delicate; semi-porcelain; no crazing
Measurements: Large tureen, 8¼" long; small vegetable, 5½" long; small platter, 6" long; tureen platter, 9½" long; plate, 6" long; butter pat, 3" long; fruit dish, 4½" long; cup, 2½" tall; saucer 4¾"
Classification: Scarce
Collection: Lechler
Price Range for Complete Sets in Good Condition: $200.00 to 375.00

Known Pattern Pieces: Tea and dinner sets for six
Point of Origin, Date: America; flare-bottom set is a Cleveland China Co. product produced by George H. Boman Company of Cleveland, Ohio, circa 1900; the round tea set with matching girls and colors is by a different American company
Colors, Ware Type, Features: Crazed semi-porcelain; fall decals of girls (outside) playing lackadaisical games and following non-essential pursuits
Identical Blanks with Different Decorations: Flare-bottom look-a-likes include children with a dachshund playing and a set of sports acitivities
Measurements: Flare-bottom teapot, 4"; sugar, 3¾"; creamer, 2½"; cup, 2¼"; saucer, 4¾"; plate, 6"; dinner platter, 7¼"
Classification: Both sets are obtainable
Collection: Baugh
Price Range for Complete Sets in Good Condition: $100.00 to 150.00 tea set; $125.00 to 165.00 dinner set

JAPANESE TEA AND DINNER SETS

Azalea (correct name)

Known Pattern Pieces: 15 piece tea set
Point of Origin, Date: Japan; Azalea marked "Noritake"
Colors, Ware Type, Features: White porcelain with Azalea motif
Identical Blanks with Different Decorations: Flag (with Nippon mark)
Measurements: Teapot, 3¼"; sugar, 2¼"; creamer, 1¾"; cup, 1¼"; saucer, 3¾"; plate, 4¼"
Classification: Rare
Collection: Lechler
Price Range for Complete Sets in Good Condition: $1,800.00 to 2,400.00
References or Author's Comments: Collectors of Azalea (adult ware) and dealers in the Azalea pattern are very eager to get this set. This has caused the price to escalate. Different designs on the same blank sell for only $45.00 to $75.00.

American Flag

Known Pattern Pieces: Tea set
Point of Origin, Date: Japan; marked "Nippon"
Colors, Ware Type, Features: Pastels on porcelain
Identical Blanks with Different Decorations: Azalea and probably others
Measurements: Teapot, 3¼"; sugar, 2¼"; creamer, 1¾"; cup, 1¼"; saucer, 3¾"; plate, 4¼"
Classification: Common
Collection: Thompson
Price Range for Complete Sets in Good Condition: $35.00 to 65.00

Birthday Party

Known Pattern Pieces: Tea set for four or six; possible dinner set
Point of Origin, Date: Japan
Colors, Ware Type, Features: Fine porcelain; pastels with gold trim; boy and girl at a table; cloth has a chain of elephants on parade; large cake on the table; quality ware
Identical Blanks with Different Decorations: See *Children's Glass Dishes, China and Furniture*, pages 144 and 145; Swan on the Lake; Ducks; Pink Roses and Bands; probably others
Measurements: Teapot, 3¾"; sugar, 3"; creamer, 2½"; cup, 1¼"; saucer, 3¾"; plate, 4¼"
Classification: Obtainable
Collection: Lechler
Price Range for Complete Sets in Good Condition: $125.00 to 200.00

Silhouettes

Known Pattern Pieces: Tea set; possible dinner set
Point of Origin, Date: Japan; Noritake; circa 1900
Colors, Ware Type, Features: Quality porcelain with black main figures; pink, black and gold border trim
Identical Blanks with Different Decorations: See *Children's Glass Dishes, China and Furniture*, page 145; Apple Blossom; probably others
Measurements: Teapot, 3¼"; sugar, 2¾"; creamer, 2"; cup, 1¼"; saucer, 4"; plate, 4½"
Classification: Obtainable
Collection: Lechler
Price Range for Complete Sets in Good Condition: $125.00 to 150.00
References or Author's Comments: Noritake stands for the company who produced the set. If a set is marked Nippon, that word stands for Japan. Dishes with Nippon marking were made from 1891 to 1921. The Noritake mark was used from 1904 to 1941. The prices of toy ware from Japan (as elsewhere) vary because of design and/or method used to achieve the desired results.

Floral

Known Pattern Pieces: 47 piece tea and dinner set
Point of Origin, Date: Japan
Colors, Ware Type, Features: Dark blue background with white floral designs; quality ware
Measurements: The ruler is 6" long in the picture, this gives the idea of the set's size; doll dishes
Classification: Rare
Collection: Schmoker
Price Range for Complete Sets in Good Condition: $325.00 to 375.00

Sports Minded Bears and Steiff Animals

Known Pattern Pieces: Tea set for six
Point of Origin, Date: Japan (this set); some sets produced in England
Colors, Ware Type, Features: Bear decals
Identical Blanks with Different Decorations: These decals appear on tea and dinner sets from Japan and on tea sets from England (different blanks)
Measurements: Teapot, 3"; sugar, unavailable; creamer, 2½"; cup, 1½"; saucer, 4³/₁₆"
Classification: Scarce because of subject matter
Collection: Hartzfeld
Price Range for Complete Sets in Good Condition: (owner priced), $275.00 to 400.00
References or Author's Comments: Steiff animals and tea or dinner sets with bears are very costly and popular at this time. Steiff Ski Rabbit named "Rico Rabbit" is 17" tall and comes complete with skis and poles for $250.00. (Without the skis and poles the price drops to $125.00.) The Steiff bear is "Zolac", producd in the 1950's. He sells for about $350.00.

JAPANESE BLUE WILLOW

Japanese Blue Willow, shown in depth in *Children's Glass Dishes, China and Furniture*, has caught the interest of collectors. Tea sets consisting of a tea pot, sugar, creamer, four or six cups, saucers and plates, are now selling for $85.00 to 125.00. The set costs about $25.00 more if the open handle cake plate is included. The larger proportioned toy sets also cost more.

Japanese Blue Willow dinner sets, if ordinary, include four or six plates, a sauce boat, a covered tureen and underplate and a meat platter. This unit costs about $125.00 to 150.00. The "Blue Plate specials" or grill plates which come in two known sizes sell for $20.00 to 30.00 per plate in either size. The oval vegetable bowl which is 5⅜" sells for about $30.00. If the grill plates and oval vegetable dishes are included in the dinner set, the price escalates to around $200.00.

The most common shape in Japanese Blue Willow is the oval. Four different sizes are shown in *Children's Glass Dishes, China and Furniture.* There may be a fifth (smaller) size. Teapots with odd shapes and/or reed handles cost more, ranging from $30.00 to 50.00 each. Red Japanese Willow or colors other than blue are more costly, no matter the size.

A table cloth and napkins called "Blue Willow" are available to buy. A set costs from $20.00 to 35.00. There is a set with the willow pattern and a set which was sold with the Willow dishes which has only the "Willow" blue (color) on white.

Some Blue Willow pieces measure as follows: (larger ones are more expensive)

creamers: 2", 1½" - $8.00 to 10.00	blue plate specials: 5", 4¼" - $20.00 to 30.00
sugars: 2", 2¾" - $10.00 to 15.00	vegetable bowl: 5⅜" - $25.00 to 30.00
cups: 1½", 1⅛" - $6.00 to 10.00	tureens: 4", 4½" (3 sizes) - $25.00 to 30.00
saucers: 3¾", 3⅜" - $2.00 to 7.00	teapots: 3¾", 2⅝" - $25.00 to 35.00
plates: 5", 4⅜", 3¾" - $8.00 to 12.00	sauce boats: only (3 sizes known) - $20.00 to 30.00
cake plates: 5¼", 4¼" - $25.00 to 30.00	

Although difficult to display, collectors are more willing to pay a higher price if boxed sets are offered for sale.

Since these sets are not very old, it might be better to put a little extra money into the old English Willow and wait until prices fall in the Japanese ware.

Top row, left to right: Three sizes of open-handled cake plates, $25.00 to 30.00 each; soup or berry bowls in front of cake plates, $12.00 to 15.00 each.

Middle row, left to right: Two sizes of divided plates or grill plates, $20.00 to 30.00; each; open (oval) vegetable bowl, $25.00 to 30.00

Bottom row, left to right: 3 sizes of covered dishes, $25.00 to 30.00 each; 3 sizes of gravy boats, $20.00 to 30.00 each

Top row, left to right: Five teapots with unusual shapes and in difficult-to-find sizes, $28.00 to 30.00 each. *Second row down, left to right:* Rare teapots with reed handles, $30.00 to 50.00 each; sets with these pots, $150.00 to 250.00 complete and mint. *Third row down, left to right:* Flat-sided tea pots in two sizes, $28.00 to 30.00 each; set, $145.00; center shows a variety of sizes and styles of creamers and two sizes of soup or berry bowls. Four sizes of the common shape teapots, the largest pot being the most difficult to find, $125.00 to 150.00 for the largest set including the oval teapot; $85.00 for other sizes of oval-shaped teapot sets. *Bottom row, left to right:* Five sizes of sugars, three sizes of cups (the largest being the most difficult to find); large berry or soup bowl; and four sizes of another style of pots which costs from $85.00 to 125.00 per tea set.

EUROPEAN TEA SETS

Scenic Pink Luster

Russian Tea Set

Pattern Name: Scenic Pink Luster
Known Pattern Pieces: Tea or coffee set for six
Point of Origin, Date: Czechoslovakia; circa 1910-1920
Colors; Ware Type; Features: Scenic view in vivid pink luster with the same luster on teapot spout and handle; porcelain
Measurements: Teapot, 5¼″; sugar, 2⅜″; creamer, 3⅛″; cup, 1⅞″; saucer, 3¾″
Classification: Scarce
Collection: Hartzfeld
Price Range for Complete Sets in Good Condition: $125.00 to 165.00

Pattern Name: Russian Tea Set
Known Pattern Pieces: Tea for one
Point of Origin, Date: Russia
Colors; Ware Type; Features: Excellent porcelain with good gold trim
Measurements: Teapot, 3½″; sugar (open handles), 2½″; creamer, 2½″; cup, 1½″; saucer, 3½″; plate, 3½″
Classification: Rare
Collection: Bobst
Price Range for Complete Sets in Good Condition: $100.00 to 125.00

The Playhouse Kitchen

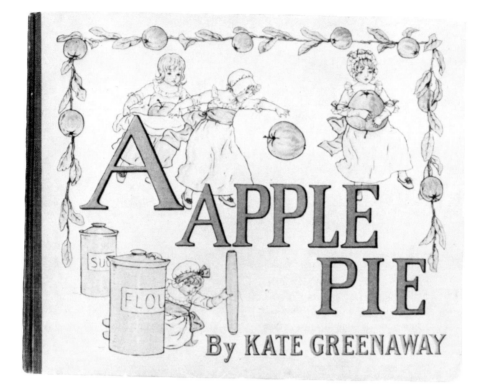

Running a playhouse was exhausting work for the little hostess, but, she was lucky. When the work became too dull or too difficult, she could turn into a child again, forsake her home and run to mother. Her bears and dolls stayed behind and behaved . . . for the most part. You will notice a bear rascal now and then in this section of the book, but usually the playhouse children did not bring in their friends and pets to run riot over a freshly scrubbed floor; nor did they eat much. One thing they did have in common with "regular" children, they didn't care to perform any of the chores around home!

It was a fortunate company, indeed, that discovered that making a miniature "like mother's" for the girls of the family could be profitable. Germany was the country that furnished us with much of our collection delights in toy forms. The early 1900's was an important time for standard size kitchen's with mom and apple pie, and playhouse kitchen's with tin and little homemakers. The world was on the brink of war and when this happened, the important German toy companies such as Bing and Marklin lost their market places.

The Marklin Company is considered to have been the best of the German toy makers with its age of toys beginning in 1859 as a family business. From 1888 the firm of Gebruder Marklin expanded steadily and was so far ahead of its time that companies and stores in competing countries simply could not keep up with their standards or innovations. Instead, these countries bought the German products, packaged them as their own, and sold them in various ways across the world. This makes it very difficult to tell where a set of items came from since most of the ware was not marked and the original boxes and packing slips have vanished as well. France bought many of ther German toy products, therefore, sets from Germany have appeared in Baskets marked France, leading people to believe that the set inside the basket also was a French product.Confusion and guessing persists today with little hope of unraveling the "origin mystery."

Marklin toys are deceptively simple, impressively assembled, and impeccably painted. This company masterfully evoked the highest quality possible and the consumers apreciated and expected it. Collectors of today enjoy the German products because they not only held up under the rigors inflicted by youth, but have lasted for us, blooming like roses in a junkyard, waiting to be displayed in show places of today.

Marklin geared itself to catering to specific markets and readily embraced new and modern methods which were needed to achieve quality production. The peak period was from 1895-1914. The demise of many companies came in the 1920's and 1930's as a result of the Great War and ensuing depression. Marklin's main set of rivals, Gerbruder Bing, Hess, Plank, and Issmayer all closed down in the 1930's.

During the "Golden Age of Toys" from 1880-1914, metal toys came into their own. These were produced by manufacturers in the Nuremberg and Wurttemberg areas of Germany. These places were traditional centers of toymaking.

You will see many of the toys in the kitchen ware section that are a direct result of the turn of the century optimism that was enjoyed in manufacturing and communications. As you look, the hours will pass in jewels, alleys, and winks of the past. Enjoy.

Kitchen Ware

Metal Tea and Housekeeping Equipage

Kitchen #1 Pewter Tea Set, in the problem section of *Children's Glass Dishes,* the butter to this set was shown. It has been found that to have a complete set, the flare-bottomed tea kettle, sugar and creamer must be bought; tea kettle, 3½″ tall and 5″ across bottom; sugar with lid 2½″ tall; creamer 2″ spout to base; butter, 2¾″ tall, 3½″ across metal base, glass dome rim, 2½″ across, collection--Lechler. Price range: $125.00 to 225.00.

Kitchen #2 Pewter Tea set, four cups and saucers, teapot, sugar, creamer, open sugar bowl, serving compote, round fruit bowl, flowers and leaves design, fancy handles, collection--Lechler. Price range: $45.00 to 75.00.

Kitchen #3 Silverplate Tea Set, child-sized tea pot, open sugar, creamer, spooner and butter dish, daisy designs, collection--Oswald. Price range: $375.00 to 600.00.

107

Kitchen #4 Doll (sized) Silver, teapot, coffee pot, creamer, sugar and tray, collection--Lechler. Price range: $125.00 to 150.00.

Kitchen #5 Housekeeping Pot Metal, salt and pepper shakers, 2″ tall; creamer and sugar, 1½″ tall; open compote, 1¾″ tall; platters, (2) 5¼″ and 4″; crumb scoop, large section, 3″, small section, 1¼″ long; ornate flower designs over the pieces; found in original box, collection--Lechler. Price range: $125.00 to 175.00.

Kitchen #6 Brass Tea Kettle and Coffee Pot, brass tea kettle has porcelain handle, 4½″ with handle straight up, base, 4¾″, from lid to base, 3½″; coffee pot with wooden handle, 5½″ tall, collection--Lechler. Price range: $75.00 to 100.00 for either.

Kitchen #7 *Cherries on Granite, tea set for six, European, circa 1890-1920; all over aqua color with vivid red cherries, teapot, 4¼″; sugar, 2¾″; creamer, 2″; cup, 1½″; deep saucer, 3″ across; rare (enameled ware was usually more expensive (when first sold) than china products in toy form) same set shown with floral decorations; French china vase, 3¾″; Straw Stuffed Bear 18″ tall, legs, 7½″ long, arms, 9″ long, shoe button eyes, black thread nose and four thread toes, had been an amber color, fully jointed, collections--Cherry Granite, Lechler; floral granite, Steffen; Bear, Knight; French Bordeaux vase, Lechler. Price range: cherry and floral tea sets, $225.00 to 325.00 each; bear, $300.00 to 400.00; vase, $25.00 to 35.00.

Kitchen #8 Cobalt Granite, tea set for six, European, circa 1890-1920; all over exterior cobalt, white interior, vertical rows of hand painted flowers accented with gold; set is commonly found in china form, but rare in enamel ware; teapot, 3½″; sugar, 2½″; creamer, 2¹/₂″; cup, 1³/₄″; saucer, 4″, collection--Lechler. Price range: $200.00 to 225.00.

Kitchen #9 *Hanging Utility Rack, rack, 5½″ tall; dipper with holes, 4½″ long; dipper with no holes, 4½″; teaspoon, 3½″, blue; krumcake skillet, blue and white, 5½″ long; creamer, blue paneled, also a complete tea set with floral decorations, 1850 to 1870, 3″ tall; spotted pan, two handles, blue and white, 1″ tall; blue and white pan, 2 handles, white interior, blue exterior, 1″ tall; pan with long handle, all blue, 1″ tall, 2½″ across, 3½″ handle; wash pan, blue exterior, white interior, 1″ tall; blue mug, 1½″ tall, 1½″ across rim; blue and white funnel, 2¼″ long; blue spoons, 4½″, 3½″; packaged enamel flatware, red handles; tea set, blue and white speckled ware, teapot, 4″; cup, 1½″; saucer, 3½″; fluted pan, ¾″ tall, 2″ across. *Bear, straw stuffed, shoe button eyes, fully jointed, 20″ long, arms, 6″ long, legs, 8″ long, long nose (up in the air); Writing Equipment, The Art of Sealing A Letter, Dennison Manufacturing Company, Mass. original wax, candles, chamberstick in brass, seal, chamberstick ¾″ tall, collection--granite ware and writing equipment, Lechler; bear, Knight. Prices ranges: utility rack and spoons, $50.00 to 100.00; krumcake skillet, $25.00 to 45.00; spotted pan, $30.00 to 35.00; blue and white 2-handled pan, $25.00 to 30.00; long-handled pan, $25.00 to 30.00; wash pan, $15.00 to 25.00; Pie spade, $50.00 to 65.00; funnel, $8.00 to 10.00; creamer, $20.00 to 25.00; blue mug, $8.00 to 10.00; packaged flatware, $10.00 to 12.00; speckled tea set, $150.00 to 225.00 complete; blue spoons, $10.00 to 20.00 each; writing box, $20.00 to 25.00; bear, $400.00 to 500.00.

Kitchen #10 Enamel Ware Stew Sets, setting for twelve, shown in navy and white and dotted spray on white, also known with floral designs, stew-plate-bowls, 3½" across; 2 round serving bowls, 3" across and 1" deep; sauce boat, 2⅝" long, 1½" tall; oval covered dish, 4" across handle; ladle, 6" long; fat stew pot, 3⅞" across handles of base, 3½" tall complete; oval platters, 5¼" x 3¼", see floral design in *Children's Glass Dishes, China and Furniture,* page 149, collection--Lechler, navy and white; Steffen, dotted spray. Price range: $325.00 to 425.00.

111

Kitchen #11 Pewter Service Set with Flatware; oval server, 3″ handle to handle; spoon, 3¼″; plates, 2¼″ (4); covered tureen, 2″ tall and about 3″ long (footed); low covered server, 1″ tall and 2¼″ long; platter, 3″ long; cup, ½″ tall; saucer, 1½″ across; knife, 4″ long; fork, 3½″; spoon, 3½″; duck knife rest (does not belong with this set), 2½″ long, collection--Lechler. Price range: $100.00 to 135.00.

Kitchen #12 Flatware and Utensils, circa 1900-1937, collection--Lechler. Price range: blue and white handled (onion style) knife, fork, and spoon, $25.00 to 35.00 per place setting; bone handled (any size) knife and fork, $20.00 to 30.00 per place setting; pewter knife, fork, spoon, knife rest, napkin ring, $4.00 to 6.00 per place setting; unknown, 20th century, metal, knife, fork, spoon, set for four $2.00 to 5.00, salt dips, $5.00 to 7.00 each; napkin ring holder in silver or pewter, $8.00; unknown metal, 50¢ each; kitchen utensils in unknown metal, 50¢ to 75¢ each.

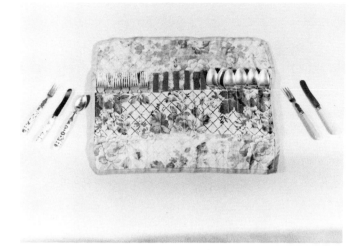

Kitchen #13 "Like Mother's" Service Set, original flatware box, collection--Lechler. Price range: $75.00 to 100.00.

Kitchen #14 Flatware Roll, original cloth roll and tie holder with place settings for six, circa 1914-1937, collection--Lechler. Price range: $30.00 to 50.00.

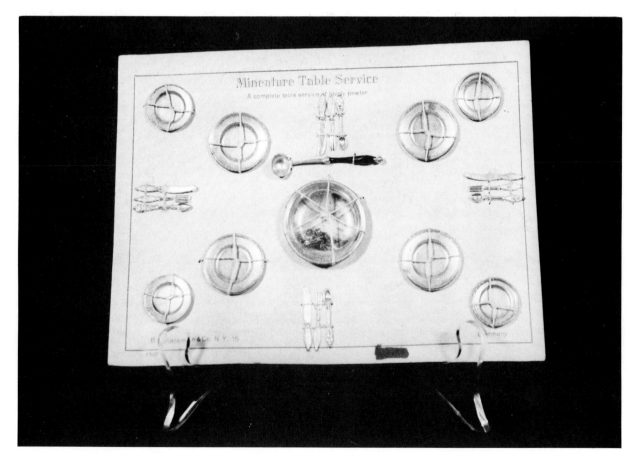

Kitchen #15 Miniature Table Service, complete table service of lovely pewter, dipper with ebony handle, Germany, collection--Lechler. Price range: $75.00 to 125.00.

Kitchen #16 Bird and Nest, hand painted tin housekeeping tea set sold in 1914, well done with lovely colors of blue, brown, green etc., collection--Lechler. Price range: set, $25.00 to 50.00.

Kitchen #17 Gray Granite Pots and Pans, child-size kitchen gray granite pots and pans, unusual in completeness, pie pan, 5¼″ across, 1″ deep; rectangular roaster, 5½″ long and 4¼″ wide; dough bowl, 4¼″ across, 1½″ deep; soup kettle with spout and handle, 4½″ across and 2″ tall; cooking pan with handle, 4½″ across and 2″ tall, 4¼″ handle; dish pan, 5″ wide and 2″ tall, collection--Lechler. Price range: $100.00 to 150.00.

Kitchen #18 White Granite Pots and Pans, navy trim around white, child-size cooking set, unusual in completeness, cooking pan with handle, 4¼″ across, 2″ tall; stew pan, 4¼″ across, 2″ tall; dish pan, 5¼″ across, 1¾″ tall; rectangular roaster, 4½″ long, 3¼″ wide; pie pan, 4¾″ across, collection--Lechler. Price range: $75.00 to 125.00.

Kitchen #19 Revere Cook Ware, covered pot, 3″; dough bowl, 3½″ across, 2″ tall; tea kettle, 4″ tall handle to base; handled pan, 3½″ across rim, 2″ tall; skillet, 4″ across, 1″ deep; toast rack, 4½″ handle to end of rack, collection--Lechler. Price range: $100.00 to 125.00.

Kitchen #20 Kitchen Equipment (group shot), collection--Lechler, back, left, brass warming dish, 4¾″ tall, $25.00 to 35.00; back, center, porcelain cookie jar with hand painting, 5″ tall, $30.00 to 50.00; back, right, French coffee grinder, 2½″, 3¼″ base; French cooking pots, wooden handles, sturdy, largest pot to smallest, 3½″ across, 2″ tall; 3¼″ across, 1¾″ tall; 2¾″ across, 1½″ tall; 2½″ across, 1¼″ tall; 2″ across, 1″ tall, pouring spouts, $150.00 to 175.00. Front, center, "Hunter's Toy Sifter, Buy A Large One, Pat. May 16, 1971-Apr. 7, 1974", 2″ highest point, $75.00 to 100.00.

Kitchen #21 Kitchen Equipment (group shot), collection--Lechler. Price range: glass jar and beater, $10.00 to 15.00; waffle iron, 3″ base, 2¼″ lid, ¾″ tall, rare size, $50.00 to 100.00; Weller crock and beater, $100.00 to 125.00; Flatware, see Kitchen #12.

Metal, Glass, Crockery and Wood

Kitchen #22 Crocks, Beater, Masher, collection--Gardner. Price range: back row, left, green crock, 2¼″ tall, 4¼″ across, $20.00 to 25.00; back, center, blue and white crock and bail, $35.00 to 45.00; back, right, kraut crock, 2½″ tall, $25.00 to 35.00; back, right end, brown slip with cream exterior, 3″ across, $50.00; front, left, yellow ware bowl with decorations, $25.00 to 35.00; potato masher, 6½″ tall, $15.00 to 20.00; nest of yellow ware bowls, 2¾″ and 1½″ tall, 2″ across and 1″ tall, 1″ tall and 1¾″ across, $100.00 to 125.00; second from right, front, sweetheart bowl (with hearts), 3″ across and 1½″ tall, $75.00 to 100.00; far right, front, brown slip bowl, $25.00 to 35.00.

116

Kitchen #23 Stone Ware Jugs, collection--Gardner. Price range: front left, white with blue bands, 1½″ tall, $20.00 to 40.00; back, left, flat-sided flask jug, 1½″ tall, $25.00 to 40.00; center, (2) tall brown jugs, 2″ high, $15.00 to 30.00 each; back, second from right, Bennington pitcher, 1¼″ tall, $45.00; back, right, gray whiskey jug, 1¾″, $20.00 to 40.00; front, right, brown cider jug, $15.00 to 25.00.

Kitchen #24: Buckets, Pins and Can, collection--Gardner. Price range: back, left, covered sugar bucket, $25.00 to 65.00; center, Droste Haarlem Holland Drostes Dutch Process Cocoa Tin, $25.00 to 45.00; back, right, $25.00 to 55.00; front, left, $25.00 to 35.00; rolling pins, $15.00 to 20.00 each.

Kitchen #25 Miscellaneous Crocks, bowls are about 2″ tall and 4″ across, collection--Hamilton. Price range: First and last bowl, $25.00 to 35.00; center bowl, $12.00 to 18.00.

Kitchen #26 Miniature Butter Moulds and Prints, collection--Gardner. Star mould, 2″ wide and 2½″ tall, $50.00 to 100.00; cow print, 2½″ base, 4″ tall, $100.00 to 200.00; leaf mould, 2″ base, 2½″ tall, $50.00 to 100.00; acorn mould, 1½″ base, 4″ tall, $50.00 to 100.00; acorn print, 1½″ base, $50.00 to 75.00; flower mould, 1½″ base, 2½″ mould, $50.00 to 100.00.

Kitchen #27 Miniature Baskets, collection--Gardner. Back row, left to right: clothes basket, 3″ tall and 5″ across, $40.00 to 50.00; melon basket, 5″ x 7″, $60.00 to 70.00; market basket, 3″ tall, 3″ across, $60.00 to 75.00; butt or gizzard, 5¾″ base to handle and 5¼″ across, $175.00 to 225.00; front right: 3 butt or gizzard baskets descending in size from 2½″ base to handle and 3″ across, 2″ base to handle and 2½″ across, 1½″ base to handle and 2″ cross, $125.00 to 165.00 each; front left: basket with egg, about 75 years old, egg is $25.00, basket, which is 4″ tall and 2½″ across is $50.00 to 75.00; front left: market basket, 2″ tall and 2″ across, $50.00 to 75.00.

Kitchen #27a Picnic Basket, tightly woven toy basket, 5¼″ handle to base, 3½″ tall without handle, 5″ long, 3¼″ wide, double entry, collection--Lechler. Price range: $100.00 to 125.00.

118

Kitchen #28 Miscellaneous Toy Products, collection--Gardner. Price range: scale, 6¾″, $35.00 to 50.00; Royal Gas stove, 4¼″ tall and 3¼″ across, $25.00 to 35.00; Pearl iron, 2¼″ tall, $28.00 to 50.00; tin lunch box, 2½″ tall, $25.00 to 35.00; sugar scoop, 3″ long, $10.00 to 12.00; tin salt box, 2½″ tall, $65.00 to 75.00; covered cup, 1¾″ tall, $10.00 to 25.00; washboard, mid-1800's, $45.00 to 65.00.

Kitchen #29 Kitchen Equipment (group shot), collection--Freshour and Lechler. French coffee grinder, 2½″ tall, 3¼″ base, $50.00 to 125.00; wall coffee grinder, 7″ long, $75.00 to 135.00; Russian urn, 1971, 5¹⁄₂″ tall, $20.00 to 35.00; tin canister or cereal set, "Farine", 3″, "cafe", 2½″; "The", 2¼″, French, $25.00 to 45.00; brass krumcake skillet, 3½″ long, $10.00 to 20.00; funnel, blue and white, 2¼″ long, $8.00 to 10.00; wooden flatware tray, 7″ long, center handle height, 2″, box height, 1½″, $25.00 to 45.00.

Kitchen #30 Multicolored Sugar Box, pewter holder with glass insert and spoon, 2″ tall, collection--Lechler. Price range: $30.00 to 60.00.

Kitchen #31 Castor Set, four bottle castor set, ring in relief around center of blown bottles, 2½″ total height, 1½″ bottle height, 1¾″ across holder section, collection--Lechler. Price range: complete with stoppers, $125.00 to 150.00.

Kitchen #32 Coffee Grinder, china section of grinder is 3″ long, wooden back is 5¾″ long, metal grinder is 1¼″ long, glass coffee catcher is ¾″ tall, white china with blue lettering, Germany, turn of the century, collection--Lechler. Price range: $75.00 to 150.00.

Kitchen #33 Wall Coffee Grinder, a bit larger than the grinder in Kitchen #32, but still a toy; toy grinders for the wall are rare, collection--Schultz. Price range: $75.00 to 150.00.

Kitchen #34 Melitta Toy Coffee Maker, Germany, factory number 801, original box, collection--Nelson. Price range: $25.00 to 45.00.

Kitchen #35 Stoves, collection--Schultz. Left to right: novelty stove in tin and cast iron, $150.00 to 175.00; Baby (has a cast iron tea kettle with slid lid), $75.00 to 125.00; tea kettle, $50.00 to 60.00; food grinder, $10.00 to 20.00; cooking pot and bucket, $12.00 to 15.00 each.

Kitchen #36 Small stoves, collection--Schultz. Back, left to right: Royal, $25.00 to 35.00; Royal, $40.00 to 50.00; Kent, $75.00 to 100.00; Eagle, $65.00 to 80.00; front row, left: Williams, $40.00 to 50.00; Geneva Champion, $35.00 to 40.00; Daisy, $25.00 to 35.00; Kilgore, $20.00 to 25.00.

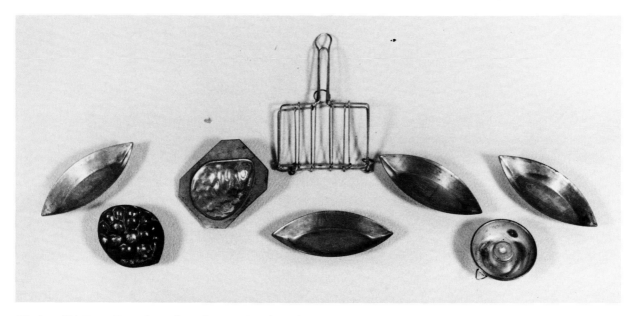

Kitchen #37 Patty Pans, boat-shaped items, 3½″ long, bumpy fruit mould, 2¼″ long (tin); strawberry mould (tin), 2½″ x 2¼″; copper mould, 1¾″ diameter; toast, fish or meat rack, 4¼″ from handle to end, collection--Lechler. Price range: patty pans, $.50 to .75 each; bumpy fruit mould, $1.00 each; strawberry mould, $1.00; copper mould, $8.00 to 10.00; toast rack, $.50 to .75

Kitchen #38 *Blue Enamel Housekeeping Set, thirteen pieces (plus lids) in original box, Bing Toy Company, Germany; pots and pans stamped Germany; original packing, never used; two handled cooker with pouring spout, 2¼″ tall and 4¼″ across spout to side; two-handled, tall pot, 2½″ tall and 3½″ across; roaster with pouring spout, 4¾″ long and 2¾″ wide; shallow, two-handled pan, 1¼″ tall and 5″ across; pan with lid, 1¾″ tall and 3¾″ across; bucket with bail, 2″ tall and 2½″ across; skillet, 1″ tall and 4″ across; two pans with handles and lids, 1¾″ tall, 3½″ across; ladles, one with holes, 5″, soup ladle, 5″; grater, 3¾″, collection--Lechler. Price range: $300.00 to 400.00.

Kitchen #39 Colander, blue and white marbled strainer with perforated bottom, two handles, 1¾″ tall, 3¾″ across, 4½″ handle to handle, collection--Welker. Price range: $100.00 to 150.00.

Kitchen #40 Blue Granite Ware, pie spade, soup dipper, strainer, dipper, about 4½″ long; grater, 3¾″ long; salt box with wooden lid; tea kettle, collection--Steffen. Price range: pie spade, $50.00 to 65.00; dippers, $25.00 to 35.00; strainer, $35.00 to 40.00; grater, $35.00 to 65.00; salt box with wooden lid, $100.00 to 125.00; tea kettle, $125.00 to 175.00.

Kitchen #41 *Blue Tea Set, see also color section; teapot, 3″; open sugar, 1¾″ tall and 1¾″ across; creamer, 1½″; cup, 1″; saucer, 2¼″ across; oval server, 4½″ long; table cloth made from handkerchiefs by Elizabeth Hall Anderson, collection--Lechler. Price range: tea set, $200.00 to 275.00 complete.

123

Kitchen #42 Blue Enamel, tea set, "Flori" Steiff lamb, collection--Steffen. Price range: $225.00 to 275.00 complete; Steiff lamb, $50.00.

Kitchen #43 Enamel Wash Pan and Water Pail, thought to be a part of a larger unit, difficult to locate this size, collection--Steffen. Price range: pail, wash pan, $150.00 to 175.00.

Kitchen #44 Lenci Doll, rare, all felt, 11″ tall, attributed to Italy, all original; spoon holder, embossed tin holder for six spoons, rare, 2″ x 3″; flour bin, unusual, this form usually is reserved for salt; utensil holder, 5″ x 2″, German, collection--Steffen. Price range: Lenci doll, $200.00 to 300.00; spoon holder, $100.00 to 125.00; flour bin, $25.00 to 35.00; utensil rack, $50.00 to 100.00.

Kitchen #45 Weller Beater and Bowl Set; pie plate, beater and bowl, another bowl, blue and white; Food Savers, (unusual size) cake, coffee, bread (not complete); 1950's mixer; all original "Teddy Li" Steiff bear, 5″ tall, collection--Steffen. Price range: Weller set, $200.00 to 225.00; food savers if complete, $150.00 to 175.00; 1950's mixer, $15.00 to 20.00; "Teddy Li" Steiff bear, rare, $200.00 to 300.00.

Kitchen #46 Cereal or Canister Set, flour, cake, bread, coffee, sugar and tea in tan with gold trim; electric (workable) Sunbeam mixer with green custard bowls, collection--Steffen. Price range: cereal set, $100.00 to 125.00 complete; Sunbeam mixer, $100.00 to 150.00.

Kitchen #47 Utensils, blue and white handled, collection--Steffen. Price range: $8.00 to 10.00 each.

Kitchen #48 Cleaning Equipment; early, rare, big-footed bear, 4″, collection--Steffen. Price range: sample rubber gloves, $8.00 to 10.00; sample cleaners, $4.00 to 5.00 each; brush set, $35.00 to 40.00; big-footed bear, $150.00 to 200.00.

Kitchen #49 "Brushes Like Mothers", "Teaches the girl to keep things clean", collection--Steffen. Price range: $20.00 to 30.00.

Kitchen #50 Dish Washing Set, red enamel dish pan; dish drainer; apron; dish towels; brushes; Vel soap and more; fully-jointed old bear, straw stuffing, mint, about 17″ tall, collection--Steffen. Price range: dish washing set, $50.00 to 75.00; bear, $300.00 to 325.00.

Kitchen #51 Corner Grocer, 15″ tall at the middle, 15″ x 8″ x 8″, packed with added merchandise, two sides fold inward, collection--Steffen. Price range: $150.00 to 200.00 complete.

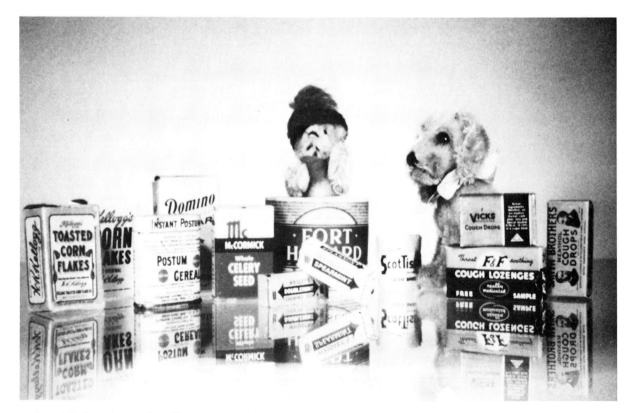

Kitchen #52 Sample Food, Kellogg's Corn Flakes, Postum, Domino sugar, Fort Howard toilet paper and others, 2″ and under in size; dog, early Stieff; bear, a German Schuko, collection--Steffen. Price range: food samples, $25.00 to 30.00 each.

Kitchen #53 Wall Coffee Grinder; Lipton, Folger's and Chase & Sanborn's coffee samples are 2″ to 3″ tall, collection--Steffen. Price range: coffee samples, $25.00 to 35.00 each; coffee grinder for wall, $125.00 to 140.00; table coffee grinder, $45.00 to 65.00.

Kitchen #54 *Bear on a Picnic, 17″ tall, 7½″ legs, 6″ arms, hump on back, straw stuffed, brown eyes, pointed nose, embroidered nose and mouth; red ware bowl with inside gray marble (type) wash; blue enamel spoons and creamer; sapphire glass tumble up; white vase crafted by Eulilia Johnson; child's picnic basket, collection--Lechler; bear, Knight. Price range: bear, $300.00 to 400.00; basket, $125.00 to 150.00; spoons, $10.00 to 20.00; creamer, $20.00 to 25.00; sapphire tumble up, $125.00 to 150.00; bowl, $25.00 to 45.00.

Kitchen #55 *Steiff Bear, ear button, straw stuffed, embroidered hands, feet and nose, shoe button eyes, fully jointed, 17″ tall, 8″ arms, 7″ crooked legs, humped back; child's miniature picnic basket; sample Pabst Blue Ribbon beer, 4½″ tall, collection--bear, Knight; other items, Lechler. Price range: bear, $800.00 to 900.00; picnic basket, $100.00 to 125.00; beer sample, $3.00 to 6.00.

Kitchen #56 *Sand Toys, enameled sand toys which could be used for mud pies and other recipes, circa 1914; yellow bear, fully jointed, leather paws and feet, amber eyes, black embroidered nose, 18″ long, 8″ arms, 7″ legs, excellent condition, collection--Knight. Price range: sand toys, $50.00 to 100.00; yellow bear, $150.00 to 250.00.

Kitchen #57 Place Card Holders, find your place at the tea table with the help of storybook characters such as Puss In Boots or Little Red Riding Hood, collection--Lechler. Price range: set of six, $12.00 to 15.00.

130

Kitchen #58 *Red Ware Churn, about 110 years old, made from one of the most popular mediums of country pottery, has a porous body with degrees of reddish-brown tones with a green slip finish; red ware usually took a utilitarian form; red ware items were made in small factories and on farms to meet everday needs; this churn has strap-applied handles and is a rare miniature with chip carved paddle and lid; jar height is 4½″ tall and the paddle-stick is 7″ long, collection--Hamilton. Price range: $150.00 to 350.00. Rolling Pin, miniature blue glass rolling pin, 4½″ long; collection--Lechler. Price range: $45.00 to 125.00.

Kitchen Furniture

Kitchen #59 Table and Chairs, round oak table with carved pedestal base, 29″ in diameter, 22″ high; flowers motif in pressed back chairs which are 11¾″ from floor to top of back and 22″ from seat to floor, collection--Lechler. Price range: $375.00 to 600.00.

Kitchen #60 Playhouse Water Bench, cherry wood, porcelain knobs, two drawers, two shelves for buckets or berry baskets, circa 1840, American; 25½″ tallest point, 15½″ shortest point, 8⅝″ deep, 23½″ long, collection--Lechler. Price range: $325.00 to 475.00.

Kitchen #61 Majestic Stove, two warming ovens, front towel bar, shelves on each side, 32″ tall; ham baking in the oven; waffle iron, Stover Jr.; coal scuttle and shovel ready for ash action; tea kettle; brass coffee pots; granite coffee pot; child's toy iron, collection--Steffen. Price range: Majestic stove, $1,500.00 to 2,000.00; bucket and shovel, $50.00 to 75.00; roasting pan, $20.00 to 30.00; tea kettle, $50.00 to 75.00; waffle iron, $50.00 to 75.00; brass coffee pots, $50.00 to 100.00 each; granite coffee pot, $100.00 to 125.00.

Kitchen #62 Grain Painted Cupboard, circa 1850-70, 32″ tall, 15″ wide; desirable piece for collectors of primitives; Steiff dog, 9″ tall, circa 1950, collection-- Steffen. Price range: cupboard, $600.00 to 700.00; dog, $50.00.

Kitchen #63 Ice Box, oak, 30″ x 13″ x 1″, brass fittings 1920-30; White Mountain Jr. ice cream freezer, collection--Steffen. Price range: kitchen cupboard, $350.00 to 550.00; ice box, $300.00 to 500.00; ice cream freezer, $100.00 to 150.00.

Kitchen #64 Oak Cupboard, frosted glass windows, spice shelf with plenty of storage room, circa 1910-1930; sample fruit jars, collection--Steffen. Price range: cupboard, $600.00 to 800.00; china spice set, $100.00 to 125.00; sample fruit jars, $5.00 to 10.00 each.

133

Kitchen #65 Bucks Jr. Stoves, two different styles, warming shelf on each, pull down shelves on each, late 1800's; two tea kettles; straw stuffed bear with shoe button eyes and fully jointed, collection--bear, stove and tea kettles, Steffen. Price range: tea kettles, $35.00 to 50.00 each; bear, $150.00 to 200.00; stove, $500.00 to 600.00; 2nd stove picture, $150.00 to 200.00; toy iron, $20.00 to 30.00.

Kitchen #66 New England Kitchen, stove, 16″ high; rare size waffle iron; bar of stove black in the oven when purchased, collection--Steffen. Price range: stove, $250.00 to 300.00; waffle iron, $75.00 to 100.00.

Kitchen #67 Tappan Eclipse, child-size gas stove; granite ware accessories, collection--Strong Museum 76.1135-78.12809. Price range: stove, $800.00 to $2,000.00; shovel, bucket, $35.00 to 75.00 each; tea kettle, $150.00; covered pan, $100.00; 3 skillets on the wall, $50.00 to 75.00 each.

Kitchen #68 Hide Chair, hickory and pine frame, original hide seat, Texas made, collected at Chappell Hill, Texas; 20″ tall, 13¼″ wide and 10″ deep, collection--Nonemaker. Price range: $350.00 to 375.00.

Kitchen #69 Dry Sink, child-size sink, 24″ tall, 14¼″ deep, 33⅓″ long; fuctional drawer and cupboard space; American; walnut, collection--Lechler. Price range: $375.00 to 425.00.

Kitchen #70 Baking Cupboard, child-size baking cupboard; American; storage bins (tin); flatware and baking storage; baking surface and glass cupboard doors; 45½″ tall; 28″ long; 15″ deep; 15½″ floor to baking surface, collection--Lechler. Price range: $800.00 to 1,000.00.

Kitchen #71 Pie Safe, pine, 19½″ x 26½″, American, bottom drawer, collection--Rogers. Price range: $225.00 to 500.00.

Kitchen #72 Ice Box, walnut, metal lined, two lids, one door, ice compartment at top, food storage on bottom shelves, about 19″ tall, collection--Lechler. Price range: $100.00 to 200.00.

The Playhouse Dining Room
Dining Room Furniture

Dining Room #1 Sideboard: mahogany; 22″ x 16″; Japanese Blue Willow tea ware, collection--Rogers. Price range: sideboard, $250.00 to 550.00; Willow tea ware, $75.00 to 100.00 (set)

Dining Room #2 Greek Revival Sideboard: rosewood; original black over brown painted graining; turned feet; 21¼″ tall; 12¾″ wide; 9¼″ depth; glass knobs, collection--Nonemaker. Price range: $350.00 to 500.00.

137

Dining Room #3 *Corner Cupboard: child-size; cherry wood; two glass upper doors; two lower wooden doors; carved skirt; 53½″ to highest point; 31¾″ upper portion; 23″ lower portion height; 33″ widest point; child's mirror on wall; children having tea; cherry frame; 14″ long, collection--Lechler. Price range: cherry corner cupboard, $800.00 to 1,000.00; cherry framed mirror, $45.00 to 75.00.

Dining Room #4 Dumb Waiter: marked "1901, Zoar, Ohio"; four tier; ball turned center post, collection--Lechler. Price range: $45.00 to 125.00.

Dining Room #5 Renaissance Revival (style) Dining Room: Philadelphia; 1865; mongram "M F" or "M J"; sideboard, 33¾" tall, 26½" wide and 8½" deep; server, 22" tall, 15¼" wide and 6" deep; (6) chairs with seat monogram, 11½" tall, 6" wide, 6" deep; oval table, 10" tall, 17¾" wide, 13¼" deep; outstanding set; collection--Mimi Findlay, New Canaan, Ct.

Dining Room #6 Sideboard: carved oak buffet; pair of lusters are Bristol glass with crystal prisms; Lechler Burmese water set; collection--Steffen. Price range: sideboard, $800.00 to 1,000.00; lusters, $375.00 to 475.00 pair.

The Playhouse Parlor
Parlor Furniture and Accessories

Parlor Furniture #1 Chair; carved, scrolled arms; walnut frame; bolster, loose pillows; rams' horns (leg) decorations; rare piece of child's toy furniture, collection--Strong Museum, card catalogue number 79.1608. Price range: $1,000.00 to 1,500.00.

Parlor Furniture #2 Automata: mechanical clockwork musical display; 1890-1912; France; bisque doll with blond wig, glass eyes ·closed, mouth red, sheer silk dress, original costume; metal key; h 39.0 x w 37.2 x 35.2 cm, collection--Strong Museum, card catalogue number 79.9584. Price range: $2,000.00 to 4,000.00.

Parlor Furniture #3 Piano and Bench; circa 1846-1901; stenciled decoupage added much later; painted black with stenciled fences, foliage, buildings and boats; cutouts of children from Greenaway's *Under the Window* (1878) and *The Tea Party* (and other pictures and rhymes for children); Mrs. Bouchey, from New Hampshire, designed and applied the decorations; hxwxd: 60.2 x 55.2 x 41; American, collection--Strong Museum, card catalogue number 76.4563. Price range: $200.00 to 300.00.

Parlor Furniture #4 Grand Piano: 19″ high (closed), 30″ high open, 19″ wide, collection--Lundquest. Price range: $100.00 to 125.00.

Parlor Furniture #5 Player Piano: marked Piano Lodeon, J.Chein & Co., U.S. and foreign pats.; plastic; usually six music rolls with each piano; made for only a short time with only a few still left in workable condition; Chein Industries, Inc. William St., Burlington, N.J. 08016; Piano Lodeon was #909; 20″ tall, 20″ wide, collection--Lundquest. Price range: in playable condition, $300.00 to 375.00.

Parlor Furniture #6 Oak Library or Fern Stand: sturdy; circa 1910-1930; two shelves; 19″ high, top is 11½″ x 11½″, collection--Hamilton. Price range: $125.00 to 165.00.

Parlor Furniture #7 French Tea Stand: early French tea table; 18½″ tall and 16½″ diameter; walnut, collection--Lechler. Price range: $300.00 to 350.00.

Parlor Furniture #8 Muffin Stand: miniature dumb waiter (style) muffin stand with silver cone finial; 16″ tall, first shelf, 7¼″ diameter, 2nd shelf, 8″ diameter, collection--Lechler. Price range: $125.00 to 150.00.

Parlor Furniture #9 Palmer Cox Brownie Frame: 2½″ picture would fit in frame; frame height (tallest point) 5½″; pin tray, collection--Lechler. Price range: $35.00 to 75.00.

Parlor Furniture #10 Toy (size) Frames: left to right: art deco jeweled frame, 3″ tall and ¹⁵⁄₁₆″ wide; turquoise hearts frame with painting on porcelain, 3¼″ tall and 2¾″ across; bevelled glass frame, 2¼″ tall and 1⅜″ across; circular frame with jet circle, collection--Lechler. Price range: $15.00 to 25.00.

Parlor Furniture #11 Framed Lithophane: candle holder attached behind frame to illuminate the picture of the child; rare collection--Mollard Antiques. Price range: $200.00 to 250.00.

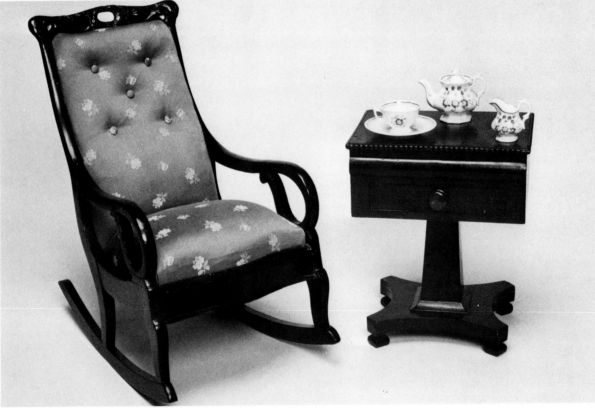

Parlor Furniture #12 Lincoln Rocker: produced circa 1865; original price tag, $65.00; walnut with a serpentine front; crest rail and finger hold; inscribed in ink on the back, "Henry Lodgegood"; heavily stained walnut; mahogany veneer; 59 x 34.3 cm., collection--Strong Museum, card catalogue number 75.125. Price range: $600.00 to 1,000.00. Night Stand: George Bulls: circa 1838: Restoration period; United States; drawer has "made by George Bulls in 1838"; 39 h x 32 l x 23.5 w, collection--Strong Museum, card catalogue number 79.1672. Price range: $350.00 to 600.00. English China: Gothic style luster ware; over glaze enamel; white body with purple luster zig-zag border; thin green band underneath; pink and yellow, purple and green; aqua flowers; see this book, "Split-Handle, Rick-Rack", collection--Strong Museum. Price range: $150.00 to 325.00.

The Playhouse Library

Library Furniture and Writing Equipage

Library #1 Wooton Desk: This is a remarkable example of the famous Indianapolis, Indiana crafter, William S. Wooton. This author uses the terms "salesman's sample" or "apprentice sample" rarely, but either term seems to fit this outstanding example of detailed workmanship. Mr. Wooton patented the "Wooton's Patent Cabinet Office Secretary" on October 6, 1874. The Wooton desk features innumerable cubbyholes, drawers and slots. The desk was made to be closed and locked each evening after the day's business was completed, collection--Strong Museum. Price range: $5,000.00 to 12,000.00.

Library #2 Fruitwood Secretary: bookcase top; fall down writing surface; two middle drawers; two door storage area at the bottom; 48″ tall; the extent of the depth of the writing area is 17½″; the desk is 29″ long, except for the crown and then it is 32″ across that surface; vase turned inset legs, collection--Lechler. Price range: $800.00 to 1,000.00.

Library #3 Oak Roll Curtain Desk: 27″ tall; 17″ deep; writing surface at full extension, 11″; shown on page 17 of *Children's Glass Dishes, China and Furniture*, but not clearly displayed, collection--Lechler. Price range: $300.00 to 450.00.

Library #4 Canterbury: revolving bookcase; English; miniature books, 3¾″ tall, include the works of Washington Irving, Shakespeare, Tennyson, Balzac, Whitman, Elizabeth Browning, Hubbard--to name but a few; bookcase is 10¼″ tall and 6″ across with a total of 18 different size book slots on its four sides; rare in miniature form, collection--Lechler. Price range: $500.00 to 700.00.

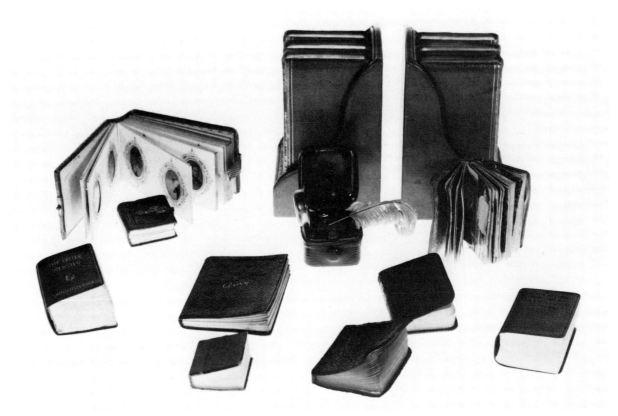

Library #5 Miniature Books and Miniature Ink Well: miniature red leather picture albums (2 known sizes given here, both are pictured) 3″ long and 1⅞″ thick; 1½″ tall and ⅜″ thick, both filled with tin-type photographs; English leather book-ends and leather bound books: dictionaries in the Midget Series (English) 4¼″ tall; miniature leather ink well and feather 1⅛″ tall, ink bottle ⅝″ tall; two diaries of little girls; dictionaries; Bibles; books from 1½″ tall to 3¼″ tall, collection--Lechler. Price range: albums, $25.00 to 35.00; bookcase book ends, $50.00 to 125.00; leather ink well and feather, $200.00; diaries, dictionaries, Bibles, $10.00 to 20.00.

Library #6 Bookrack: English bookrack with stenciled ends; entire book-filled rack is 10″ long; books in miniature are 3¼″ tall; works of Shakespeare (20 books), sterling silver desk set: sealer, 3½″, roller, 4½″ letter knife, 4½″, collection--Lechler. Price range: book filled rack, $100.00 to 150.00; sterling silver writing set, $150.00 to 275.00.

Library #7 Pewter Desk Set: ink well holder complete with lids, 3⅛″ long, 1¼″ tall; blotter rocker, 1¾″ long; pen tray, 3¼″ long; pen, 2¾″ long, collection--Lechler. Price range: $225.00 to 250.00.

Library #8 Lap Desk Collection, back, left to right: suitcase desk with pens and bottles; English; front falls down; 6¼″ tall, 8⅛″ wide, 4″ deep. Price range: $225.00 to 300.00. Slat-Front: center; lift for storage, also, ink and pen rack; 9″ long, 4¾″ tall at highest point; French china ink bottle and rack; also, sterling ink well. Price range: lap desk, $125.00 to 150.00; French china ink well set, $75.00 to 85.00; sterling ink well, $15.00 to 20.00. English Lap Desk: back, right: red leather interior trimmed with gold; English crest on outside center; ink bottle, stamp and pen compartment; 8½″ long, 3¼″ tall. Price range: $100.00 to 125.00. Slate-Slant: front, left: lift top with changeable card holder (6 different lesson cards); all original parts include ink bottle, pen wipe (shown on outside lid) set of envelopes and six instructional cards with 12 lessons; slots and compartments arranged for easy use; 11¼″ long, 3¾″ tall at highest point, 1¾″ at lowest point. Price range: $150.00 to 175.00. Ink Box: front, right: English; 3 compartments for stamps, ink bottle, pen wipe whiskers; 5½″ long, 2″ tall at highest point, 3″ deep. Price range: ink box, $75.00 to 100.00; collection--all of Library #8, Lechler.

Library #9 Portable Desk: miniature lap desk; very small and complete; 8.1 x 13.2 x 5.7 (h); rare size; circa 1900; hinged cover opens to compartmentalized sections with colorless ink bottles with loose covers (2) separated by stamp box with loose cover; in the back is space for other writing paraphenalia; made of wood, metal, velvet and nickel plate, collection--Strong Museum, card catalogue number 79.2665. Price range: $225.00 to 325.00.

Library #10 Thonet Desk Set: oak, double-seat set; platform base; #12612, page 91 in Thonet Brothers catalogue of 1904; Dover; height, 21½", 47¹/₂" wide and 18" deep, collection--Mimi Findlay of Canaan, Ct. Price range: $500.00 to 1,200.00.

147

The Playhouse Bedroom and Grooming Equipment

Bedroom Furniture

Bedroom #1 Oak Washstand: 21″ tall from floor to top of back, 19½″ wide, 13″ deep, four drawers and a bonnet box, glass knobs, American; Chamber Set: see chamber sets, Grooming Accessories #9 and #13 in this publication; pitcher, 3¾″ tall; bowl, 2″ tall and 4⅜″ across; potty, 1¾″ tall; toothbrush case, 3″ long; sponge box, 2″ long, floral design, collection--Schmoker. Price range: oak washstand, $425.00 to 650.00; chamber set, $150.00 to 200.00.

Bedroom #2 Empire (style) Fainting Couch: inlaid stars and bows, ornamental fret work, covered in red velvet, walnut wood, child-size, 16½″ highest point, 8½″ lowest point, 32¾″ long, 20″ wide, collection--Lechler. Price range: $800.00 to 1,000.00

Bedroom #3 Pine Fainting Couch; pine frame, walnut legs with sausage turnings, 13¼″ tall, 32¼″ long, 14½″ deep, collection--Nonemaker. Price range: (owner priced), $395.00 to 625.00.

Bedroom #4 Mule Chest: lift top, one fake drawer at top, two long drawers, original brown over yellow painted graining, 24⅞" tall, 25" wide, 12¼" deep, collection--Nonemaker. Price range: (owner priced), $750.00 to 1,150.00.

Bedroom #5 Empire Chest: shallow scrolled front, black and red painted graining, 18¼" tall, 16½" wide, 10¾" deep, collection--Nonemaker. Price range: (owner priced), $450.00 to 550.00.

Bedroom #6 Tramp Art Chest with Mirror: 16¼" tall, 8¾" wide, milkglass pulls, popular form from 1860's to 1930's, mediums were: chip-carved wood, cigar boxes, orange crates; cigar boxes or orange crate materials were used by carving V-cuts or U-cuts (gouged out) or a zigzag pattern, stained dark, pieces were applied to cover exposed areas by gluing or nailing them in pyramidal layers, collection--Ruth E. Smith. Price range: $200.00 to 300.00.

Bedroom #7 Tramp Art Dresser: 13" to top of mirror, 9½" wide, one large and three small drawers, designs of roses and leaves cut into wood, crafted by wanderers or tramps who "tramped" the land looking for work; this craft evolved from a European tradition of chip-carving wood for decorative purposes; the carver used every day forms, translating ideas to chip-carved wood, cigar boxes or orange crate material, collection--Ruth E. Smith. Price range: $225.00 to 325.00.

Bedroom #8 *Playhouse Dressing Room: what-not stand in walnut, 37″ tall with four shelves; toy tea sets shown and described in *Children's Glass Dishes, China and Furniture*: top and bottom shelves (two different sizes of same ware), page 164, top left; shelf two, page 160, top left; shelf three, page 161, top left; Larkin (style) desk: 34″ tall, 9⅛″ deep, 26″ long, oak, cupboard for dresses, two drawers and a bonnet or wash set compartment, drop-down writing surface; brass (child's) hat rack: 45½″ tall; quilt by Elizabeth Hall Anderson; doll hats created from abandoned 1930's hat shop--all old material used in these creations by Linda Gardner; Victorian (child's) purses above what-not stand, collection--Lechler. Price range: walnut what-not, $275.00 to 375.00; Victorian red velvet purses, $80.00 to 90.00 each; Larkin (style) desk, $450.00 to 600.00; brass hat rack, $75.00 to 125.00; hats, $25.00 each.

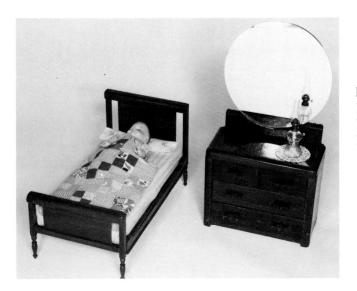

Bedroom #9 Art Deco (style) bedroom suit: bed, 26″ long, head 14″ high and 14″ wide; dresser, floor to mirror, top, 29″ high, 16″ wide, 8″ deep, collection--Lundquest. Price range: $50.00 to 100.00.

150

Bedroom #10 Fashion doll: circa 1880, France, bisque head with swivel neck, kid body, 38 cm., grey-blue blown eyes, closed mouth, pierced ears and earrings; trunk is black with brass trimmings, collection--Strong Museum, card catalogue number 74.2753. Price range: trunk, $150.00 to 200.00; doll case with accessories, $75.00 to 300.00.

Bedroom #11 Trunk: attributed to Germany, circa 1903-1920, wood, leather, 28h x 40.5l/w x 24d (measurements in cm.), (see Strong card catalogue number 80.4667); wood trunk covered with alligator, trimmed with brass hinges, compartments inside with separate tray--all covered with paper and pictures of the time, collection--Strong Museum. Price range: $200.00 to 400.00.

Bedroom #12 Carret Trunk: manufactured by Carret, circa 1900, France, wood, artificial leather (cover), brass trim, cloth covering inside, 39.6w x 31.4h x 24.8d (see Strong card catalogue number 73.369), collection---Strong Museum. Price range: $150.00 to 300.00.

Bedroom #13 Umbrellas for Play: #1: chantilly lace over white taffetta, carved ivory handle serving dual purpose as a scent bottle, ivory tip, 7″ handle, 2½″ tip, 20½″ tip to tip; #2 double covering on circular frame, ebony-colored fold-up handle, scalloped black material edges, 18″ long; #3 black silk with faint brown stripe, fringe, wooden handle, 19″ long; #4 taffetta under-layer with organdy tip-puff and extra decorative layer, fold-up handle, 20″ long, collection--Lechler. Price range: #1, $150.00 to 200.00; #'s 2-4 from $45.00 to 65.00 each.

Bedroom #14 French Washstand: circa 1903, legs come apart to adjust to height of user, towel bar on each end, tilt mirror, collection--Steffen. Chamber Set: five pieces in this lavishly decorated set include bowl, pitcher, potty, toothbrush holder and soap dish unit, collection--Steffen. Price range: French washstand, $300.00 to 400.00; chamber set, $125.00 to 150.00.

Bedroom #15 Bedroom Suite: circa 1920's, a gift to a little girl in Stillwater, MN, on Christmas Eve; straw hat on dresser is one of twelve sample straw hats; dressing table holds two miniature birthday candles, a hair receiver, hatpin holder, ring tree, and powder jar; comb, brush, mirror and powder box and puff with the little handle...the original box is stored carefully in the drawer, collection--Steffen. Price range: bedroom suite, $300.00 to 425.00; dresser set, $50.00 to 135.00.

Grooming Accessories

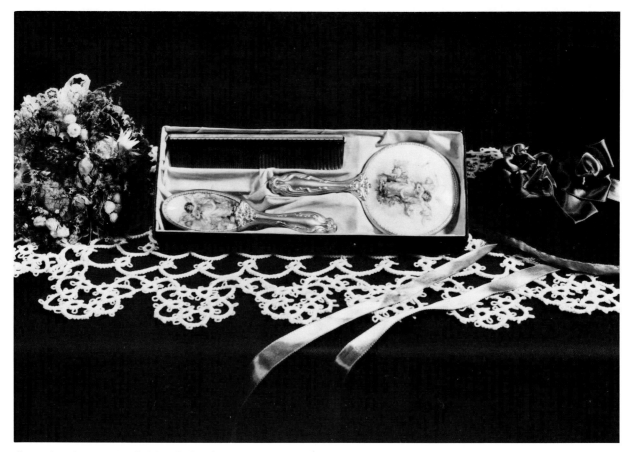

Grooming Accessories #1 *Comb, brush, mirror in original box, hand painting on porcelain, girl in long dress standing on a leaf; mirror, 6″; brush, 5½″; comb, 6″; lavish gold handles and rims; handwork by Ruth E. Smith, collection--Lechler. Price range: grooming set in original box, $125.00 to 150.00.

Grooming Accessories #2 Brass brush, mirror, pomade box, brush, collection--Lechler. Price range: $45.00 to 75.00.

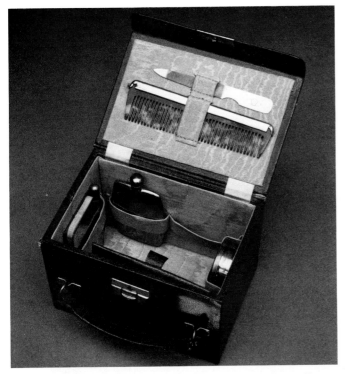

Grooming Accessories #4 *Doll's bath tub in metal holder: basin, white enamel with hand painted violets, complete height, 16¼", tub length, 18¼", collection--Lechler. Price range: $150.00 to 300.00.

Grooming Accessories #3 English travel grooming kit, collection--Strong Museum, card catalogue number 79.324. Price range: $45.00 to 75.00.

Grooming Accessories #5*French china in a wooden washstand: washstand height, 18"; washbowl, 15¼" length; pitcher height, 10"; soap dish, 4¾"; blue transfers on white ware of children and puppets; marked "K & G Luneville France", collection--Lechler. French Kate Greenaway (style) Wash Set; produced by Utzschneider & Co., marked "Sarreguemines"; circa 1890-1901; Sarreguemines pottery was made in Germany during the 18th century and later in France by Utzschneider & Co.; this company made much soft paste ware, biscuit figures, stoneware and majolica; wooden stand which is 18" tall; washbowl, 15¼" long; transfer printing on cream-colored earthenware; see another version in the book *Children's Glass Dishes, China and Furniture*, page 21, collection--Strong Museum. Price range: French china in washstand, $600.00 to $1,000.00; Kate Greenaway Wash Set, depending on condition and number of pieces, $600.00 to 1,200.00.

Grooming Accessories #6 Chubu China Dresser Set: Chubu china, made in occupied Japan, circa 1945, Nippon quality with lavish gold accents on porcelain with tiny hand painted flowers; tray, 3½" long; powder jar, 1"; stoppered bottles, 1½" tall, collection--Lechler. Price range: $75.00 to 125.00.

Chamber Sets and Dresser Equipage

Grooming Accesories #7 *Black Bird: This unusual chamber set consists of six pieces. One piece has an unknown function and is 1½" tall and 1¾" across. It carries a single black bird with cream, light blue and pink which are also shown in the rest of the set. The bowl is 2" tall and 5¾" across. The interior shows seven black birds. The water pitcher is 4¾" from lip to base and has six black birds and the word "Depon" and "2228" hand painted on the base. The 4" long covered box with air holes has three black birds. The 2½" long box with air holes has only two birds. The potty to this set is 1¾" tall and 2¾" across the opening. It has two birds, collection--Lechler. Price range: $300.00 to 325.00.

Grooming Accessories #8 Buster Brown: This unusual toy set was found at an advertising show in its original box along with the packing slip. This set consists of five pieces. The pitcher, which is 5″ in height, shows Buster Brown and his dog. Buster is carrying an American flag. All of the pieces are trimmed with gold. The interior of the wash bowl shows three children and a dog in a pillow fight. The bowl is 2¼″ tall and 6¼″ across the rim. The toothbrush box is 4¾″ long and shows a spanked Buster in the corner with the dog in wait. The hairbrush is also in evidence. A covered box, shorter than the toothbrush container shows two children and the dog running. This box is 3″ long and still contains packing bunting. The potty, which is 2″ tall and 3″ across, shows Buster (in pink) running with his dog. Nearly all of the pieces carry a hand painted number 36, collection--Lechler. Price range: $350.00 to 500.00.

Grooming Accessories #9 Blossoms and Gold: This chamber set includes five pieces. The flowers are light pink. Gold enhances the split-handled pitcher as well as the counterparts. The pitcher is 3¾″ tall. The bowl is 2″ tall and 4⅜″ across. The potty is 1¾″ in height. The toothbrush case is 3″ long and the sponge box is 2″ long, collection--Lechler. Price range: $150.00 to 200.00.

Grooming Accessories #10 Orange Berry: This set is about half the size of the other chamber sets in this division. There is an orange band with hand painted flowers emphasizing each member of this five-piece assemblage. Berry finials completes this porcelain unit, collection--Sembric. Price range: $75.00 to 125.00.

Grooming Accessories #11 Fluted Toilet Set: This set is one of the most complete on record. The Strong Museum displays this eight-piece set in their museum. The card catalogue number, 79.2459, describes this child-size toy as having a white background with yellow shading. The fluted body has rim scallops. The covered pieces have flower finials rimmed with gold. The flowers are purple with green leaves on all of the pieces. There is a chamber pitcher and bowl, a powder jar, a cotton jar, a sponge dish and a soap dish. There is also a waste bowl complete with holes. The set has overglaze painting, collection--Strong Museum. Price range: $300.00 to 375.00.

Grooming Accessories #12 *Wedgwood's functional, child-size pitcher and bowl set is trimmed with burgundy elegance. The pitcher is 6″ tall from lip to base. The bowl is 2½″ tall and 8″ across the rim. "Wedgwood Pearl" is impressed on each of the bases. Circa 1840-1868, collection--Lechler. Price range: $150.00 to 175.00.

Grooming Accessories # 13: *top row, left to right:* *Fall Leaves: the measurements for this chamber set are the same as Grooming Accessories #9, collection--Lechler. Price range: $150.00 to 200.00; Ropes of Roses, petite designs of flowers on light green background, located in its original box, same measurements as Grooming Accessories #9, collection--Lechler. Price range: $150.00 to 250.00. *Bottom row, left to right:* Gemma (marked), Goss (type) toy dresser set, several interesting accessories, all with colorful crests, tray, 6″ long, candlesticks, 2½″ tall, ring tree, 1¼″, large pomade, 1½″, short pomade, ¾″, collection--Lechler. Price range: $125.00 to 175.00; Toy Three-Way Mirror, little girls in the "Florence" style, 4″ tall, collection--Lechler. Price range: $25.00 to 40.00; Blue Blooms, set is trimmed by heavy gold, five-piece chamber set found in original box, pitcher, 5″ tall, bowl is 1½″ tall and 5½″ across, soap dish is 2¼″ long, potty, 2″ tall and 2½″ across rim, toothbrush box, 3¾″ long, collection--Lechler. Price range: $150.00 to 225.00.

Grooming Accessories #14 Scenic Square: this set is similar to the sets in the group photo. This set's uniqueness is due to the scenic square in the center of a leaf and flower design. There should also be a potty in this set. The pitcher is 5½″ tall, the bowl is 2″ tall and 5¾″ across, the toothbrush dish is 3½″ long, the soap dish is 2½″ long, collection--Lechler. Price range: $150.00 to 200.00.

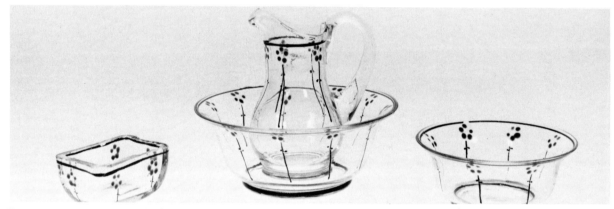

Grooming Accessories #15 Glass Chamber Set: bought in England, circa 1800's, found four pieces, clear glass with hand painted blue flowers with gold accents, rare find, pitcher, 3¼″; large bowl, 1¾″ tall and 4¼″ across; small bowl, 1½″ tall and 3¼″ across; rectangular dish, 2″ long and 1¼″ across, collection--Lechler. Price range: $225.00 to 325.00.

Grooming Accessories #16 European Enamelware: rare wash set in toy form, pitcher, lip to base, 4¼″; bucket base height, 3¼″; bucket hole filler, 4″ across; toothbrush holder, 4¼″; soap dish, 2¾″; bowl, 2⅛″ tall and 6¼″ across, all over white enamel with aqua spray accent; chamberstick, blue, with original box of matches, 2½″ tallest point without match box; match box marked, "British Made Bryant & May's, BryMay special safety match", 1¾″ long; chamberstick saucer, 2½″, collection--Lechler. Price range: wash set, $225.00 to 325.00; chamberstick, $125.00-150.00.

Grooming Accessories #17 *back row, left:* Ewers and basins, luster, gold, blue, orange-brown and green, also available with yellow in place of all the green, 5¼″ from base to handle, diameter of bowl is 4¼″; *back row, middle:* luster, blue, orange, green, yellow, ewer height is 5¼″ from base to handle top, bowl is 5″ across; *back row, right:* mocha trimmed with black lines, ewer height is 5″ from base to handle top, bowl is 4¾″ across; *front row, left:* pink luster, orange-brown, green, yellow, ewer is 3¾″ from base to handle top, bowl is 4″ across; *front row, right:* blue luster, gold, blue, orange-brown, green, ewer is 4½″ from base to handle top, bowl is 4½″ across, collection--Ruth E. Smith. Price range: $125.00 to 150.00 per set. Comment: Spode was known for their miniature ewers and basins. These items are well potted and were made in the early 1800's. Their purpose was mainly decorative rather than functional.

Grooming Accessories #18 *left to right:* Ewers and basins, luster, gold, blue, orange-brown and yellow, ewer height is 5¼″, bowl is 4¼″ across (same set as group picture Grooming Accessories #17, the first one, back row, left); *middle:* cobalt, mustard, green on white, slim and graceful, ewer is 3¾″ from lip to spout, saucer-like basin is 4¼″ across; *end:* black, lavender, red, yellow, gold, ewer height is 4″ spout to base, basin is 1¼″ tall and 4¼″ across, collection--Lechler. Price range: $125.00 to 150.00 per set.

Grooming #19 Sandwich, pitcher and basin, pitcher is 2″ tall, bowl is 1″ tall and 3¼″ across, collection--Lechler. Price range: $125.00 to 200.00.

The Playhouse Laundry and Sewing Equipment

Laundry Equipment

Laundry #1 Toy Columbia Washing Machine, circa 1900-1914, rotary, sold with adult counterpart by the Sears Roebuck Co. in 1909, collection--Eisele. Price range: $225.00 to 325.00.

Laundry #2 Toy Wash Stand, wringer mounted on toy wash stand, wash tubs and rinse water section; toy clothes rack, circa 1900-1914, collection--Steffen. Price range: washstand, $50.00 to 125.00; rack, $20.00 to 45.00.

Laundry #3 Wee Washer, circa 1914, collection--Steffen. Price range: $75.00 to 100.00.

Laundry #4 Sunny Suzy Washing Machine, circa 1914, collection--Steffen. Price range: $30.00 to 40.00; Steiff Bear and Washing Equipment, collection--Steffen. Price range: rack, $10.00 to 20.00; basket, $10.00 to 25.00; bear, $100.00 to 125.00.

Laundry #5 Tuesday is ironing day, collection--Steffen. Price range: irons, $25.00 to 30.00; starch sample, $10.00 to 20.00.

Laundry #6 Iron Grouping: *left to right*: Slug (heater or log) iron, made of iron or steel, this box iron is heated by an insert called a "slug", 4", collection--Schultz. Price range: $65.00 to 85.00; Mondragon, charcoal iron, cast iron, probably European, 3¾", collection--Schultz. Price range: $60.00 to 80.00; Gas (or alcohol), probably not a child's iron, but used as such, 5" plus tank, collection--Schultz. Price range: $150.00 to 175.00; Charcoal, possibly German, 3¾", collection--Schultz. Price range: $150.00 to 175.00; Kendrick, toy box iron, possibly English, 3⅛", collection--Schultz. Price range: $160.00 to 190.00.

Laundry #7 Iron Grouping: *left to right:* Potts Iron, often sold by the weight--14 to 20 ounces, listed as a toy or a child's iron, 3¾" long, collection--Schultz. Price range: $35.00 to 55.00; Potts, not listed as a toy, but used by children, 5" long, collection--Schultz. Price range: $35.00 to 55.00; G.F. Ober, Chagrin Falls, Ohio, pat. 1895, 4" long, collection--Schultz. Price range: $50.00 to 75.00; Sensible, made by the Streeter Company, circa 1887, 4⅛", collection--Schultz. Price range: $50.00 to 75.00; Sad Iron, iron produced by Reuben J. Meyers, an ad for this iron may be seen in a Butler Bros. 1895 catalogue, sold in lots of four dozen or more, $1.90, 4⅜" long, collection--Schultz. Price range: $60.00 to 80.00; White City, sad iron, Potts (type), 3¾" long, collection--Schultz. Price range: $35.00 to 55.00. The Pearl, 3¾" long, collection--Schultz. Price range: $30.00 to 50.00. Reference: *Tuesday's Child* by Politzer, priced by Schultz.

Miniature Sewing Machines

Anything that revolutionized the adult household was quickly made into a lesson-teaching device for the little homemaker. At the turn of the century, toy model machines made from heavy sheet steel or cast metal came onto the market. Germany was once again ahead of the trade world in this miniature category. Not until the 1930's and 1940's were the machines produced in any great number in the United States. The greatest majority of miniature sewing machines came from the United States, Germany, Japan and England. The ads from these countries stressed the dual role of the miniature sewing machine, emphasizing that the adult as well as the child could benefit from the machine's countless wonders. Some were chain or gear driven while later models ran on electricity.

Sewing Machine #1 Black enamel with beautiful flowers in red with gold trim cover this nickel-plated beauty from the early 1900's. This is probably a German creation. Price range: $50.00 to 75.00.

Sewing Machine #2 This is a Casige sewing machine from the British zone of Germany. It sews a chain stitch and is only one of several Casige choices. Price range: $100.00 to 125.00.

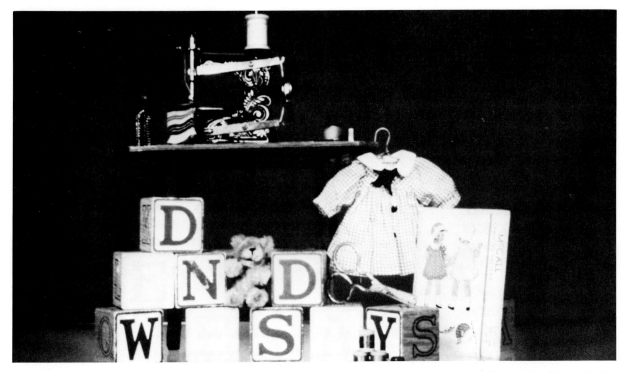

Sewing Machine #3 The little American seamstress did her mending on Wednesday, according to the blocks in this picture. This is another black enamel, heavily decorated example of childhood quality products. The bottle on the left is a sample of three-in-one sewing machine oil. There are toy thimbles for little sewers--one thimble has the engraving "for a good girl." The pattern is a miniature McCalls copy, collection--Steffen. Price range: machine, $45.00 to 75.00.

Sewing Machine #4 This old miniature sewing machine is chain driven. Price range: $45.00 to 100.00.

Sewing Machine #5 Baby Brother was made in Japan. An electric motor drove this "baby". Price range: $35.00 to 65.00.

Sewing Machine #6 Singer produced this machine around 1910-1914. Black enamel was the popular finish for miniature machines. Price range: $45.00 to 60.00.

THE IDEAL SEWING MACHINE.
No. 1.

A Child's Companion and Instructor.

A Useful Assistant to every Mother.

Simple and solid in its construction, perfect in its operation, so easy to run that every child can work it readily and satisfactorily.

So neatly and perfectly does it do its work that every lady will find it to be thoroughly practicable for all plain sewing, and of great convenience and assistance in the household.

No. 1 Ideal Japanned and Nickel-Plated Sewing Machine, height to top, 25 inches; extreme height, 31 inches; length, 18 inches; width, 12 inches.

$4.25 Each.

Sewing Machine #7 The Ideal Sewing Machine, No. 1 ad illustrates how the machine "is a useful assistant to every mother." Price range: $100.00 to 125.00.

Sewing Machine #8 This "Singer" machine was produced in England. The numbers show the little seamstress how to thread this new invention. Price range: $35.00 to 75.00.

Sewing Machine #9 Kayanee was powered by two flashlight batteries. This hardwood-base machine was produced to last, in Germany. Price range: $50.00 to 100.00.

Sewing Machine #10 Sewmaster was produced in Germany after World War II. Decorated with flowered decals, this model is only one of several Kayanee's produced. Price range: $45.00 to 100.00.

The Playhouse Porch and Lawn Furniture

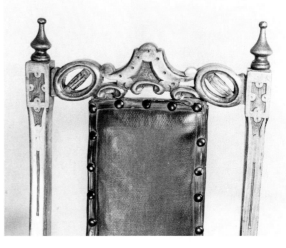

Lawn Furniture #1 Folding Lawn Chair, walnut, carved, country version of Renaissance Revival style, back splat and seat in black leather, circa 1870, 28″ high, 14½″ wide, 24″ length, collection--Mimi Findlay, New Canaan, Ct. Price range: $200.00 to 400.00.

Lawn Furniture # 2 Wicker Settee, original color wicker, tight weave, sturdy, seat for two children, 31″ wide, 22½″ tall, collection--Sembric. Price range: $350.00 to 450.00.

Lawn Furniture #3 Wicker Porch Furniture, white wicker, fancy-back chairs, sturdy, small tea table, collection--Lechler. Price range: $275.00 to 375.00.

Lawn Furniture #4 Wicker Luncheon Set, 25½″ x 18½″, 20″ high table, chairs, 24″ high, collection--Lundquest. Price range: $275.00 to 375.00.

Lawn Furniture #5 Wicker Love Seat, original weave, seat for two, collection--Private. Price range: $300.00-385.00.

169

Miniature Glass

Beverage Sets, Table Ware, Miscellaneous Glass

Beverage Sets (priced per complete unit)

Miniature Dishes #1 Mary Gregory, amber toy beverage set, two tumblers with boys in white turned in one direction, two girls on the other (two) tumblers turned in an opposite direction, pitcher, 4½″, tumblers, 2½″, known also in blue, collection-- Lechler. Price range: $600.00 to 800.00.

Miniature Dishes #2 Strawberries, tankard (type) pitcher, 5¼″, tumblers, 2¼″, this set is shown in *Children's Glass Dishes, China and Furniture,* pages 60 and 61 with forget-me-nots and lily-of-the-valley, more difficult to locate with strawberries, although all designs are scarce, collection--Lechler. Price range: $225.00 to 325.00.

Miniature Dishes #3 Petite Hobnail, water pitcher, 4¼″, tumbler, 2³⁄₁₆″, tumbler to the water set and tumble up are the same, also, the hobnails and product in general are obviously from the same company, tumble up known in "sandwich blue", water set known in clear and blue with a matching tray, tumble up jug, 3¾″ tall, collection--Lechler. Price range: water set, $380.00 to 425.00, tumble up, $400.00 to 425.00.

Miniature Dishes #4 Jacobean, doll's house water set in original box, made in Czechoslovakia, jug, 1½″, tumbler, ¾″, collection--Lechler. Price range: $125.00 to 150.00.

Miniature Dishes #5 Birds and Flowers, English lemonade set in child-size, clear glass with all over frosted pink surface enhanced by heavy enamel work featuring black and white birds and lily-of-the-valley in relief, pitcher 5½″, tumbler, 3¾″, collection--Lechler. Price range: $150.00 to 275.00.

Miniature Dishes #6 No. 15091 Toy Water Set, United States Glass Company product shown in the 1910 catalogue, design looks like a band of almonds, "Optic" is perhaps the name given this set, pitcher, 4″, tumbler, 2″, collection--Lechler. Price range: $75.00 to 100.00.

Miniature Dishes #7 Pattee Cross, punch cup not shown in *Children's Glass Dishes* or *Children's Glass Dishes, China and Furniture*, correct bowl is still in question, punch cup with sharp petals, 1¼″ tall and 1½″ across, collection--Lechler. Price range: cup, $25.00 to 30.00 each.

Miniature Dishes #8 Tumble Ups, over-shot, Heidelberg with clover, 2¾″ complete; blue dots, 2½″ complete, collection--Lechler. Price range: $125.00 to 150.00.

Miniature Dishes #9 *Tumble Ups, sapphire with handle, 4″ tall complete, 3″ jug, 2″ handled tumbler, brilliant blue with heavy enameled flower, leaf and vine design in pink, green, yellow, orange and light blue, collection--Lechler. Price range: $250.00 to 350.00; Moser, covered box and tumble up to match, might have been a part of a toy dresser set, green glass encrusted with gold and enamel, tumble up, 2¾″ complete, box, 1¾″ tall, pastel enamel, collection--Lechler. Price range: tumble up and box, $375.00 to 475.00; ornate cranberry, tumble up, 4¼″ complete, jug, 3½″, tumbler, 2″, cranberry glass with lavish quilted enamel and gold, pastel colors of enamel--yellow, lavender, green and white, collection--Lechler. Price range: $600.00 to 650.00; tumbler, misplaced in picture taking, another example of the Mary Gregory (Miniature Dishes #1) water set, this tumbler is blue with gold trim on the base roping, girl is different as well, 2½″.

172

Miniature Dishes #10 Tumble Ups, Mary Gregory, three sizes, three examples (two of which have been shown before), *left to right*, cobalt, 1½″, cranberry or apple green, 3⅛″, canary, 4¾″ (tumbler has boy picking flowers, jug has girl holding flowers), collection-Lechler. Price range: cobalt, $350.00, cranberry or apple green, $350.00, canary, $450.00.

Miniature Dishes #11 Clear Decanter and Tumbler, decanter, 2″; tumbler, 1⅛″ (attributed to Sandwich); Moser green tumble up with gold and enamel trim, 2¾″ complete, collection--Largent. Price range: clear glass decanter and tumbler, $150.00, Moser tumble up, $350.00 to 400.00.

Miniature Dishes #12 Tumble Ups, clear etched, American tumble up, 5″ complete, jug, 2¾″, tumbler, 1¾″; English blown glass tumble up, 1½″ complete, collection--Lechler. Price range: either, $15.00 to 25.00.

Miniature Dishes #13 *Tumble Ups, amethyst, *top, left*, 5⅜″ tall, plain with mould created panels, collection--Lechler. Price range: $150.00 to 200.00; *Moser *top, middle* two Moser tumble ups, one in aqua, 2¼″, one in blue, 2½″ extensive enamel and gold work on both, collection--Lechler. Price range: $350.00 to 375.00 each; *Du Berry, pink glass pitcher, 4¼″ with 2¾″ tumbler, fitting inside neck of pitcher, black handle, rare example, collection--Lechler. Price range: $300.00 to 375.00; *Ornate Cranberry, tumble up, 4¼″ complete, jug, 3½″ tumbler, 2″, cranberry glass with lavish quilted enamel and gold, collection--Lechler. Price range: $600.00 to 650.00; *Pink Cased, jug with ruffled lip, art glass tumble up complete, 3½″, yellow enamel design which looks (like) gold over the main sections, collection--Lechler. Price range: $325.00 to 400.00; *"Sandwich Blue" Tumble Up, see information Miniature Dishes #3, jug, 3¾″ tall and the tumbler is 2³⁄₁₆″ in height, collection--Lechler. Price range: $400.00 to 425.00.

Miniature Dishes #14 Tumble Ups, yellow cased glass, cup with handle (unusual feature), gold swirl painted design, yellow-white marble (type) glass, jug, 3½″; handled cup, 2¾″, total height, 5¼″, collection--Lechler. Price range: $175.00 to 225.00; Mary Gregory, canary tumble up, 4¾″ tall, collection--Lechler. Price range: $450.00; Clambroth, gold-ringed trim on clambroth, 3″ complete, 2¾″ jug, 1½″ tumbler, collection--Lechler. Price range: $150.00 to 175.00; *Sapphire With Handle, 4″ tall (see Miniature Dishes #9), collection--Lechler. Price range: $250.00 to 350.00; *Cobalt, swirl (in the mould) pattern, rough pontil on both the pieces, 5″ complete, collection--Lechler. Price range $100.00 to 125.00; *Nailsea, unusual three piece miniature tumble up set in swirled design, tumble up 3¼″ complete, jug, 3″, tumbler, 1¾″, plate, 3¾″ across, Nailsea, made in both England and Scotland, was an off-shoot of bottle industry, mid-19th century, collection--Lechler. Price range: $600.00 to 800.00; *Blue Etched, yellow handle on the 4¼″ pitcher, flower etching on both pieces, tumbler, 2¼″ tall, 5″ complete, collection--Lechler. Price range: $300.00 to 325.00; *Flare-Bottomed, cobalt glass with enameled art work, 4½″ complete, 3″ across base, collection--Lechler. Price range: $300.00 to 350.00.

Miniature Dishes #15 German decanter Set, decanter, 5″ complete with stopper, footed glass, 1¾″, tray, 5¼″ across, frosted glass with gold trim, collection--Lechler. Price range: $125.00 to 175.00.

Miniature Dishes #16 Leaf and Grape Decanter Set, five pieces including a tray, 5¾″ across, decanter, 5½″ complete, another stoppered bottle, 3½″ footed goblet, 2″, covered jar, 2¾″, clear glass with etching, collection--Lechler. Price range: $225.00 to 375.00.

Tableware

Miniature Dishes #17 Block Table Set, Large Block comes in amber, blue or clear, a blue milkglass creamer has been seen, but to date no other members of the milkglass unit; butter, 3″; sugar, 4½″, creamer, 3″; spooner, 3″; all pieces are difficult to locate, collection--Lechler. Price range: butter, $55.00 to 75.00; sugar, $45.00 to 75.00; creamer, $30.00 to 45.00; spooner, $40.00 to 60.00.

Miniature Dishes #18 Button Arches, quality glass from Duncan Miller, butter, 3¾″, 5″ across butter base, spooner, 2⅛″ tall, 2″ across rim, creamer, collection--Lubberger and Johnston. Price range: butter, $100.00 to 150.00; sugar, $75.00 to 100.00; creamer, $30.00 to 45.00; spooner, $45.00 to 65.00.

Miniature Dishes #19 Plain Pattern #13, see *Children's Glass Dishes, China and Furniture*, see page 99, known in crystal, cobalt, clear with frosted panels, white opalescent, collection--Johnston. Price range: (opalescent ware) butter, $100.00 to 125.00; sugar, $100.00 to 125.00; creamers, $50.00 to 65.00; spooner, $50.00 to 75.00.

Miniature Dishes #20 Stippled Loops, butter only, stippled loops with a diamond design in each loop, pleated lid rim, collection--Schmoker. Price range: $75.00 to 100.00.

Miniature Dishes #21 Long Ribbons, flint covered dish is just a possibility at this point, butter, 2⅝″, 3⅜″ across base rim, no other members of a table set unit have surfaced, collection--Lechler. Price range: butter, $35.00 to 45.00.

Miniature Dishes #22 Cup-Creamer, creamer looks as though a pouring spout has been added as an after thought, poorly made glass with excess material on several spots, pineapples alternating with stemmed plant, 12 pineapples on the creamer, no other members of this pattern have surfaced, collection--Lechler. Price range: creamer, $5.00 to 7.00.

Miniature Dishes #23 Pickle Caster, miniature pickle caster complete with glass, holder and tongs, rare, collection--Schumaker. Price range: $325.00 to 375.00.

Miniature Dishes #24 Cobalt American Shield, caster set in cobalt, see *Children's Glass Dishes, China and Furniture* for other caster sets, rare, collection--Schumaker. Price range: $300.00 to 375.00 complete.

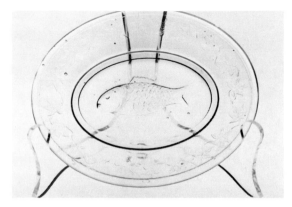

Miniature Dishes #25 Fish Platter, Federal Glass Company's main platter to the fish series, same set as the A B C ice cream set except the center picture has changed from ice cream to fish 5¼″ long, 4½″ wide, small round plate, 2¾″ diameter, collection--Lechler. Price range: main platter, $275.00 to 300.00; small, round, $75.00 each.

Miniature Dishes #26 French, Verreries De Portieux, 23 pieces were shown on a page from a French 1894 catalogue, (two) blue goblets, two green opalescent goblets (also known in clear), #4082, 1¾″ tall, cup and saucer, #4062, 1¼″ tall cup, saucer, 2½″ across, double dip dish, #4072, 2¼″ long, ¾″ bowl height, 2″ center handle top to base, light blue decanter, #34070, 4½″ tall, bowl, #4068, clear, 1″ tall and 1½″ across, collection--Lechler. Price range: tumbler, $8.00 to 10.00; double dip, $15.00 to 18.00; decanter, $20.00 to 22.00; cup and saucer, $20.00 to 25.00; bowl, $10.00 to 12.00. French, Verreries De Portieux, group shot of clear French miniatures only two of which are shown on the 1894 catalogue picture known to this author, age of this grouping is in question, covered sugar is #4080, open compote is #4075, (both of which are shown on the catalogue page), collection--Steffen. Price range: creamers, $5.00 to 6.00; sugar, $8.00 to 10.00; cup and saucer, $10.00 to 15.00; compote, $10.00 to 12.00.

Miniature Dishes #27 Epergne, true miniature at 4″ tall, three sections, base alone is 1½″ tall and 2½″ across, second section, 2½″ tall and 1¾″ across, top horn, 2¼″ long and 1″ across; lavish gold clock, 5⅝″ tall, collection--Welker. Price range $300.00 to 350.00; clock, $200.00 to 300.00.

Miniature Dishes #28 Custard, epergne, 6″ tall, 3″ at base's lowest point, horn, 4¾″, no decoration, collection--Lechler. Price range: $125.00 to 150.00.

Miniature Dishes #29 Single Piece Epergne, 3½″ tall, sterling base, glass flower-shaped horn, zippered stem, collection--Lechler. Price range: $45.00 to 75.00.

Miniature Dishes #30 Epergne blue glass, 8″ tall, enamel decoration in white and orange on blue glass, collection--Lechler. Price range: $100.00 to 125.00.

Miniature Dishes #31 Epergne, green opalescent, fire-lights when held to the light, poorly decorated with white flowers, have seen one with excellent daisy decorations, 6¼″ tall, collection--Lechler. Price range: $75.00 to 125.00.

Miniature Dishes #32 Cake, Muffin Stands, Lacy Dewdrop cake stand, also known in a mug in miniature, Lacy Dewdrop banana stand, 4⅛″ tall and 7½″ long, Paris muffin stand, (cake stand and banana stand also available in Paris pattern), 3¼″, collection--Lechler. Price range: $35.00 to 40.00 each.

Miniature Dishes #33 Glass Baskets, possibly Fenton, cherries with wire handle and no paint, 4¼″ across and base is 1″ tall; daisy design with hand painting, collection--Lechler. Price range: $12.00 to 20.00.

Miniature Dishes #34 Bride's Basket, aqua to white with very good gold trim on the interior, leaf work in the base of the holder, 2½″ tall and 4¼″ diameter, collection--Schmoker. Price range: $125.00 to 150.00.

Miniature Dishes #35 Ice Cream Cone Holder, "depression green" glass, 2½″ tall, 1½″ across, see other cone holders in *Children's Glass Dishes, China and Furniture,* collection--Lechler. Price range: $38.00 to 45.00.

Miniature Dishes #36 Ivy Ball, miniature, 2¾″ tall, amber, used for ivy cuttings and hall greenery, collection--Lechler. Price range: $75.00 to 85.00.

Miniature Dishes #37 Jardiniere, pink luster, base is 3⅞″ tall and 2¼″ across top, urn is 2¼″ x 2¼″, beaded trim area is gold, collection--Schmoker. Price range: $50.00 to 100.00.

Miniature Dishes #38 Vases, frosted glass with green frosting on upper part and enamel decoration, 2″ tall, crystal glass with gold decorations, 4″ tall, all over stippled frosting with gold rim trim, 4″ tall, collection--Lechler. Price range: $20.00 to 25.00 each.

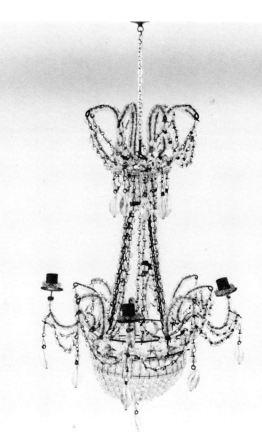

Miniature Dishes #39 *Miniature Chandelier, one of a pair with tin candle cups, 11″ tall with four candle cups, collection--Lechler. Price range: each, $375.00 to 500.00.

Miniature Dishes #40 Art Glass Milk and Mush Set, attributed to Moser, cranberry decorated, decorated with raised enamel flowers, bowl is 2½″ across, pitcher is 2″ tall, collection--Schmoker. Price range: $225.00 to 350.00.

Miniature Dishes # 41 Novelty Dish, sapphire, wording in base "Merry Christmas", holly design, 4¾″ across, not counting the handles, 1½″ tall, collection--Lechler. Price range: $50.00 to 75.00.

Miniature Dishes #42 *Dutch Boudoir, set consists of: pitcher (girl with jug), 2¼″ spout to base; bowl (three children, 1½″ tall and 3⅛″ wide; potty (Dutch girl with long braid), 1⅜″ without the lid; candlestick (reproduced by Mosser, marked with "M" in blue milkglass, amber and red), 3″ tall; waste jar (Dutch boy), 2⅛″ without lid; tray (impressed Dutch children), 6″ long, 3⅝″ wide at middle; pomade jars with metal tops, 1¾″ tall with cap; blue or white milkglass, green or crystal, the green is a "Depression Green", very rare in green or crystal, collection--Welker. Price range: green or clear glass sets, $1,000.00 to 1,200.00; blue or white milkglass, $700.00 to 850.00; milkglass pitcher, bowl, $100.00 to 125.00; green or clear pitcher, bowl, $300.00 to 350.00; milkglass tray, $300.00 to 350.00; green or clear tray, $500.00 to 600.00; old milkglass candlestick, $125.00 to 150.00 each; green or clear candlestick, $200.00 to 300.00 each; milkglass pomades (2), $200.00 to 225.00 complete; green or clear pomades (2), $300.00 to 400.00 complete.

Sandwich Attributions

Sandwich Glass Miniatures

Those afflicted with a mania for attributions have caused two overly worked and ill-used labels which plague collectors of today: "Sandwich" and "salesmen's samples". Sandwich is a generic rather than a specific description which sheds a dim light on a factory, a location, and a period of time between 1825-1888. The label "salesmen's samples" can be tossed from this catagory completely because drummers simply were not a part of the Sandwich glass spectrum during the time when miniatures were produced at the Boston and Sandwich Glass Company. Furthermore, the standard Sandwich glass and the miniature Sandwich glass have little or nothing in common when the patterns are compared.

Whether a genius or simply a man completely in tune with his chosen profession, it is clear that Deming Jarvis was remarkably good at his job. The Jarvis memory has cast a spell of glory over a particular segment of American glass. Prices and stories continue to grow grand as the image is romanced. In reality, very little is known about the man who founded the Sandwich glass works other than he guided his plant for thirty years and then set up another establishment only a half mile away which was called the Cape Cod Glass Company.

Boston and Sandwich Glass Company produced nearly every type of glass during its sixty three years of business. The keen judgment of Deming Jarvis, honored by an association with the New England Glass Company, caused the selection of an advantageous spot for his Sandwich glass works. It seems that then and now, the Boston and Sandwich enterprise was ranked with the best--the New England Glass Company and the Bakewells of Pittsburg.

Sandwich was famous for its lacy table products, flint glass lamps, spills, and candlesticks in colors that thrill the hearts of collectors. Miniature collectors were not left out. There were: tureens and trays, creamers, cups and saucers, oval vegetable dishes, round bowls, footed hexagonal bowls, larger footed bowls, miniature plates, candlesticks and chambersticks, pitchers and bowls (a mint set in cobalt sold for $900.00 at a 1984 auction), rectangular-shaped footed dishes, flat irons, tumblers, caster bottles, and compotes.

The wonderful Corning Glass Museum sent several pictures of Sandwich Glass miniatures for your enjoyment. Jane Spillman and the office and library staff have been a great help throughout the years with their unselfish displays of aid to researchers and friends of the museum.

Sandwich #1 Sandwich (attributions) pitcher and bowl set, pitcher, 2″ spout to base; bowl, 1″ tall and 3¼″ across; compote, 2″ tall and 1¾″ across; candlestick (questionable origin, could be Sandwich, French or of mid-west origin), 2¾″ tall and 1¼″ across base; tumbler, 1½″; goblet in clear, blue or green, 1¾″ tall; relish, 3″ long, collection--Lechler. Price range: pitcher and bowl, clear, $150.00 to 250.00; compote, $200.00 to 225.00; candlestick, $150.00 to 175.00; tumbler, $10.00 to 20.00; goblet, $5.00 to 8.00; relish, $145.00 to 175.00.

Sandwich #2 Plate, colorless glass, probably Boston and Sandwich Glass Company, Sandwich, Ma., circa 1835-1850, diameter, 5.7cm., collection--Corning Museum of Glass. Price range: $75.00 to 100.00.

185

Sandwich #3 Cup and Saucer, colorless glass, probably Boston and Sandwich Glass Co., Sandwich, Ma.; circa 1835-1850, cup and saucer height, 3.0 cm.; cup rim, 3.4 cm.; saucer diameter, 5.7 cm., glass rod cluster handle, collection: The Corning Museum of Glass. Price range: $200.00 to 300.00.

Sandwich #4 Cup and Saucer, colorless glass, probably Boston and Sandwich Glass Co., Sandwich, Ma., circa 1835-1850, cup and saucer height, 3.3 cm.; cup rim diameter, 3.2 cm.; saucer diameter, 4.9 cm., collection--The Corning Museum of Glass, gift of Mr. and Mrs. H. Snyder. Price range: $200.00 to 300.00.

Sandwich #5 Covered tureens in colorless glass and opaque glass, see also the color section, probably Boston and Sandwich Glass Co., Sandwich, Ma, circa 1835-1850, tureen height with cover and tray, 5.7 cm., length, 6.7 cm. (colorless set), opaque light blue glass set, tureen height with cover and tray , 5.8 cm., length, 7.9 cm.; tray width, 4.9 cm., length, 6.8 cm., collection--Corning Museum of Glass. Price range: colorless, $300.00 to 450.00; color, $500.00 to 900.00.

Toy Glass Mugs

Glass Mugs will be described from left to right:

Glass Mugs #1 Boy With Begging Dog, crawling boy on the reverse side, 3½″ x 3″; Swan, feathers around bottom, the neck and head form the handle, 3½″ x 2¾″, collection--Schmoker. Price range: $25.00 to 35.00.

Glass Mugs #2 Mercury, For a Good Boy, leaf motif, the vacant interiors of these toy mugs were silvered with a solution of bismuth, lead, tin and mercury. The mixture was poured into the mugs through a small aperture, shaken to coat the insides and then the excess liquid was poured out. The hole in each mug was sealed to protect the inner surface from the atmosphere, collection--Schmoker. Price range: $55.00 to 65.00 each.

Glass Mugs #3 Clear Arches, beaded handle, busy design, 3″ x 2¾″; Cut Log (type), good glass, 3″ x 2½″; Palm Leaf Fan, reference Kamm, book II, page 63, 3″ x 2½″, collection--Schmoker. Price range: $30.00 to 45.00.

Glass Mugs #4 Draped, gold trim, gold handle, 3″ x 2″; Clear Stippled, ball and beaded trim, beaded handle, 3½″ x 2¾″; Lacy Dewdrop, beads and stipples, flounced base, 3″ x ¾″, reference Metz, book 1, page 192, collection--Schmoker. Price range: left, $12.00; center, $45.00; end, $45.00.

Glass Mugs #5 Rose In Snow, with roses and stippling, 3½″ x 3″, marked "In Fond Rememberance", U.S. Glass Co., a touch of green, 3¼″ x 2¾″; Remember Me, large size, clear front lettering, stippling, 3¼″ x 3¼″, collection--Schmoker. Price range: $35.00 to 50.00.

Glass Mug #6 Garfield & Lincoln, historical, clear or blue, 2½″ x 2½″, collection--Schmoker. Price range: $100.00 to 125.00.

Glass Mug #7 Garfield, dated 1880, collection--private. Price range: $50.00 to 75.00.

Glass Mugs #8 Flower Band, two rows of squares, 2½″ x 2½″, with or without saucer; Flint Historical, similar to three shields, heavy glass, 2½″ x 2½″; Cherry, clear glass, 2½″ x 2¼″; Diamond Band, 2¼″ x 1¼″, collection--Schmoker. Price range: $35.00 to 65.00.

Glass Mugs #9 Hobnail, amber, blue or clear, twist handle, 3″ x 2½″; Floral Twigs, stippled, amber, six-pointed design in base, 3¾″ x 3″; Log and Star, amber, 2¼″ x 2″, collection--Schmoker. Price range: $35.00 to 65.00.

Glass Mugs #10 Flare-Bottom Squares, clear amber, blue, 2½″ x 1¾″, In Fond Remembrance, amber, clear, 3½″ x 3″, stippling, collection--Schmoker. Price range: $25.00 to 40.00.

Glass Mugs #11 Soda (type), 3½″ x 2″, United States Glass Co., Kansas pattern; Swirl With Beaded Handle, 3¼″ x 2½″; Ice Cream Soda (type), low, smooth handle, 3¼″ x 2½″, United States Glass Company, collection--Schmoker. Price range: $10.00 to 12.00.

190

Glass Mugs #12 Etched Flower and Cherubs, garlands, applied handle, blown barrel shape, 3¼″ x 2″; 89th birthday, 1894, clear with applied handle and etched age and date, collection--Schmoker. Price range: $35.00 to 65.00.

Glass Mugs #13 Etched Red Riding Hood, possibly Crystal Glass Co., see *Children's Glass Dishes, China and Furniture* for more etched mugs, page 75 (M-1, M-2) and page 76, (M-5), 3″ x 3½″, collection--Johnston. Price range: $75.00 to 100.00.

Toy Glass Plates

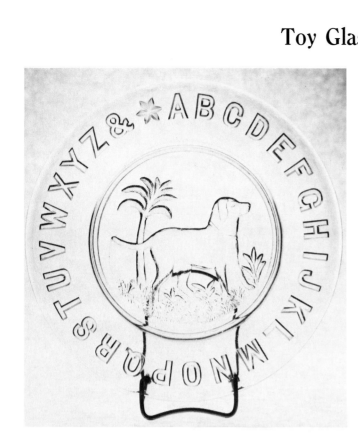

Glass Plate #1 Proud Dog, A B C border. Price range: $28.00 to 38.00.

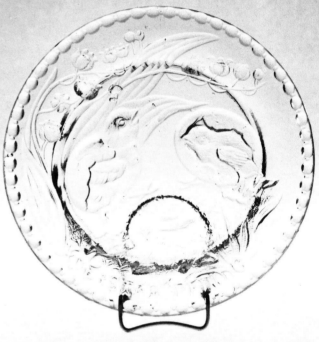

Glass Plate #2 Baby Chicks. Price range: $20.00 to 30.00.

Glass Plate #3 Duck and Rabbits, heavy milkglass, painted, gold border, collection--Private. Price range: $35.00 to 50.00.

Glass Plate #4 Rabbit and Alphabet, possibly Crystal Glass Co., 6″ diameter. Price range: $28.00 to 38.00.

Glass Plate #5 Ducks and Alphabet, possibly Crystal Glass Co., 6″ diameter. Price range: $28.00 to 38.00.

Glass Plate #6 Stork and Alphabet, possibly Crystal Glass Co., 6″ diameter, collection--Johnston. Price range: $38.00 to 58.00.

Informational corrections for the glass section in the book *Children's Glass Dishes, China and Furniture*:

Acorn, pages 33 and 34: Attributed to the Crystal Glass Company.
Baby Thumbprint, page 36: There is another compote which is open, having a flared rim.
Liberty Bell, pages 70, 71: Adams and Company produced the miniatures rather than Gillinder and Sons.
Little Jo, page 72. The old sets also came in a "Depression pink".
Nursery Rhyme, pages 94 and 95. A green punch cup with a lid was purchased with a green Dutch Boudoir set.
Petite Hobnail, pages 98 and 99. There is a tumble up which uses the same tumbler as the water set.
Plain Pattern No. 13, page 99: This set also comes in white opalescent milkglass.
Mason jar, page 112: Instead of Bell, it should be labeled Ball.

Miniature Candlesticks in Glass, China and Metal

China Candlesticks and Chambersticks #1 Pastel flowers on the first and fifth chamberstick in this picture, green flowers and leaves with burnished gold trim, also, pink and tan flowers with gold, 1¾″ tall, saucer base 3½″, collection--Lechler. Price range: $30.00 to 40.00 each; Biscuit baby on a leaf, pastel colors, little girl holding a tulip-shaped flower which is the candle cup, 2¼″ tall with a leaf-saucer at 3¼″ long, collection--Lechler. Price range: $50.00 to 75.00; Dresden with spring flowers in a shell-shaped saucer, 1½″ tall, 2¾″ from handle to other side, collection--Lechler. Price range: $30.00 to 40.00; Porcelain candlestick, one of pair, 3″, white, collection--Lechler. Price range: $25.00 to 35.00 pair.

The main body of candlesticks and chambersticks is shown in my books *Children's Glass Dishes* and *Children's Glass Dishes, China and Furniture*. In this publication, additional selections in glass, china and metal are presented. Because the glass sticks were numbered from the beginning, that particular numbering system is retained beginning with C-49. The C#'s pertain to glass tapers and the MC #'s refer to metal chambersticks or candlesticks.

C-49 Long tears around the base, paneled stem and under rim, 2½″ tall, known in clear, collection--Lechler. Price range: $30.00 to 35.00 each.

C-50 Candlestick, 1860-1880, line and ball base, excess glass, poorly finished, interesting miniature because point of origin is argued, 2¾″ tall, base, 1¼″ diameter, collection--Lechler. Price range: $175.00 to 185.00.

C-2 Four-branch candelabrums, very rare, actually three branches with four candle cups, 4¾″ center post, 4″ outer branches, two views, collection--Lechler. Price range: $100.00 to 150.00 each.

MC #1 English pewter chambersticks, 1½″ tall, 2″ base diameter, collection--Lechler. Price range: $125.00 to 150.00 a pair.

MC #2 English silver candlestick, 3¾″ tall, collection--Lechler. Price range: $75.00 to 100.00 each.

MC #3 Elf-handled chamberstick #02088, silver plate, collection--Lechler. Price range: $35.00 to 45.00 each.

MC #4 Sterling #354, curled leaf handle, 1½″, collection--Lechler. Price range: $45.00 to 55.00 each.

MC #5 *Back left:* Simpson, Hall, Miller & Co., quadruple plate chamberstick, ornate rim decorations, 2¼″ tall, 3″ base, collection--Lechler. Price range: $25.00 to 35.00.

MC #6 *Back middle:* English, sterling candlestick, one of a pair, 3¾″ tall, collection--Lechler. Price range: $100.00 to 125.00 a pair.

C-51 *Back right:* Mercury glass candlestick, one of a pair, 3¾″ tall, collection--Lechler. Price range: $120.00 to 135.00 a pair.

MC #7 *Middle left:* English, (2) copper saucers with brass candle cups and finger rings, first (middle row), 1½″ tall, second (middle row), 1″ tall, both have 2½″ saucers, collection--Lechler. Price range: $35.00 to 75.00 each.

MC #8 *Middle row, third from left:* Merden Silver Plate Co., quadruple plate, lion holding a vase crest, #02087, 2¼″ tall, waving seaweed design with a leaf and vine finger ring, collection--Lechler. Price range: $25.00 to 35.00.

MC #9 *Middle row, right:* English, metal, gold in color, attached candle snuffer (megaphone-shaped), heart-shaped chamberstick, 1½″ tall, ¾″ snuffer, collection--Lechler. Price range: $75.00 to 125.00.

MC #10 *Front, center:* Pansy (shaped), pot metal (type) chamberstick, one of a pair, Englsih, ½″ tall, collection--Lechler. Price range: $20.00 to 35.00 each.

C-52 Bristol, glass, blue candlesticks, ¾″ tall, collection--Lechler. Price range: $25.00 to 40.00.

Miniature Accessories and Christmas Stocking Stuffers

Miscellaneous Accessories #1 Maison Huret No. 22 Boulevard Montmartre Paris, an advertisement in miniature, china bowl secure in a metal stand, collection--Strong Museum, card catalogue number 77.10513. Price range: Unknown.

Miscellaneous Accessories #2 Syrups or warm milk pitchers, parts of complete china sets, 3½″ in height, there are collectors of miniature syrup pots, collection--Lechler. Price range: (each) $35.00 to 40.00.

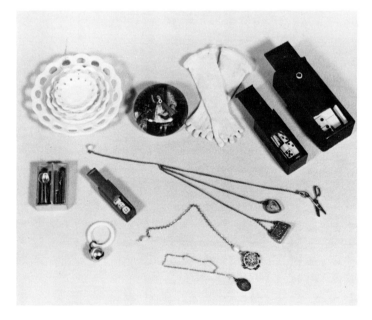

Miscellaneous Accessories #3 Accessory Grouping: back row left to right; nest of serving dishes, white porcelain with arcading, possibly German, 3½″, 2¼″, 2″, 1½″, collection--Lechler. Price range: $10.00 to 12.00; Miniature paper weight, Red Riding Hood, knocking at Grandmother's door, English, collection--Lechler. Price range: $25.00 to 50.00; Opera Gloves, doll's gloves, 3½″ long, original box, collection--Lechler. Price range: $15.00 to 20.00; (2) Rosewood boxes, sliding lids, miniature ivory dominoes, 3¼″ box, 1″ dominoes, 2¼″ box, ½″ dominoes, collection--Lechler. Price range: $50.00 to 75.00; Middle row, left to right: Silverware, divided wooden box, 1½″, knife, 1¼″, fork, 1¼″, spoon 1⅛″, collection--Lechler. Price range: $12.00 to 15.00; Miniature dice box, 1½″, slide top, walnut, collection--Lechler. Price range: $10.00 to 20.00; Chatelain, toy, gold metal, collection--Lechler. Price range: $50.00 to 100.00; front row, left to right: Teething ring, bell, collection--Lechler. Price range: $5.00 to 8.00; Toy dress watch, circa 1914, collection--Lechler. Price range: $18.00 to 30.00; Miniature rosary, 3½″ long, English, pink and blue beads, collection--Lechler. Price range: $50.00 to 100.00.

Catalogue Pages of Toys

Toys

Shape number 316 | Dutch Toy Jug.
317 | London Shape, Toy, Handled Cup, Saucer and Can.
318 | Ball Shape, Toy Teapot, Sugar and Milk.
319 | Low, Toy, Teapot, Sugar and Milk. *2 sizes*
320 | Toy Jug on a foot.
321 | Bute, Toy, Handled Teacup and Saucer. *2 sizes*
322 | Toy Can. *2 sizes*
323 | Common Shape, Toy Cup. *larger size. 'made for London May 18th 1815'*
324 | Fly-Handled, Covered Toy Can with Turned Down Stand.
325 | Vase Shape, Toy Coffeepot.
326 | Common Shape, Toy Cup and Saucer. *2 sizes*
327 | Dutch, Toy Ewer.
328 | Déjeuner Paris Toys.
329 | Toy Slop Bowl.
330 | Toy Cup made for T. Richards. *4 sizes*
331 | Toy Chamber. *2 sizes*
332 | Bow-Handled, Toy Bucket. *2in.*
333 | Antique, Toy Jug and Stand.

Catalogue #1 Josiah Spode was famous for blue printed earthenware, having perfected the process about 1790. His son, using ideas taken from illustrations in books of the time, created well known examples of country scenes. An excellent example of Spode's work is shown in the English dinner ware section of this book. The set is called "Tower". The pictures on this set are based on the Bridge of Salaro, near Porta Salara, from Merigot's "Views of Rome and its Vicinity" (1798). The border found on "Tower" is also found on another famous Spode creation called "Milkmaid".

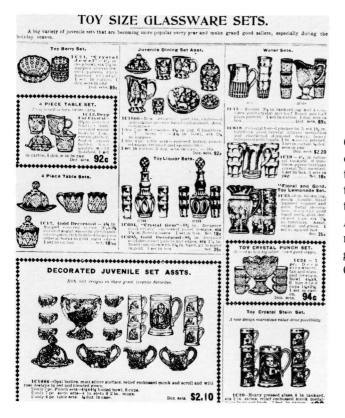

Catalogue #2 Butler Brothers was the one of the largest distributors of glass ware and china in America. This wholesale firm boasted thirty-two acres of floor space in just two of their buildings. The products that passed through this company give us an excellent sampling of the entire market. Some of the catalogue reprints are available from: Antiques Research Publications, P.O. Box 9361, Chattanooga, Tennessee 37412. This catalogue example shows a variety of toy size glassware (sets) most of which were produced by the United States Glass Company in the early 1900's.

Catalogue #3 This catalogue page illustrates a number of bears and stuffed toys available in 1910. A Teddy Bear buying guide is listed as an aid to new collectors:

--fully jointed head, arms and legs

--straw stuffing inside the six bags that represent the bear's being

--covering of the six straw stuffed bags should be a mixture of cotton and wool called mohair

--arms should be long and curving with tapering paws which extend to the bear's knees

--felt pad paws are in order

--long, slim feet are a desirable attribute for bears; the length of the bear's feet to his height is in a ratio of 1:5

--the nose, mouth and four claws on each paw should be embroidered; rust, deep brown or black floss is considered acceptable

--a small head with a long pleasing snout is best

--a pre-1912 Steiff bear in black or white is considered quite nice

--a bear's condition should be as pristine as possible

Reference: *Teddy Bears and Steiff Animals* by Margaret Mandel.

200

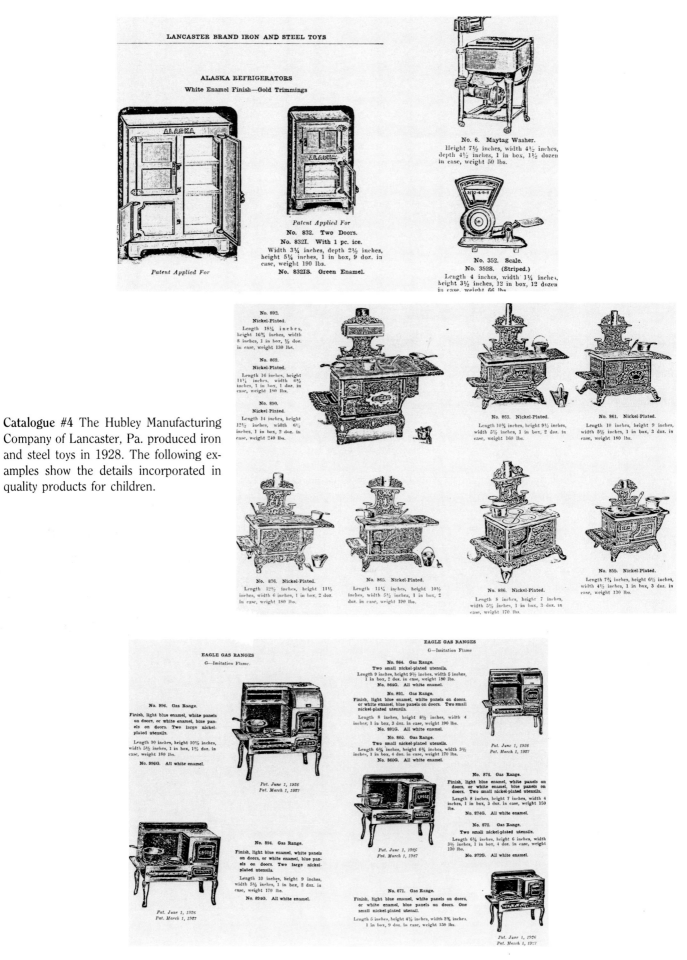

Catalogue #4 The Hubley Manufacturing Company of Lancaster, Pa. produced iron and steel toys in 1928. The following examples show the details incorporated in quality products for children.

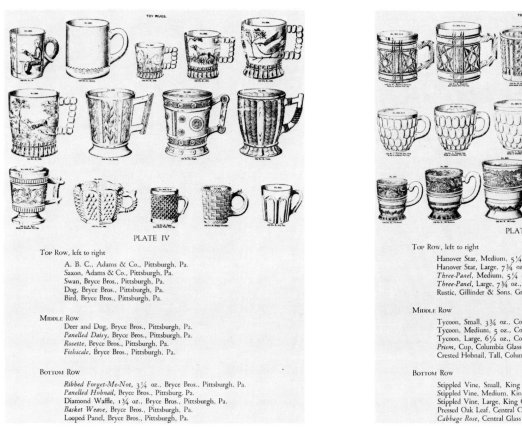

PLATE IV

Top Row, left to right

    A. B. C., Adams & Co., Pittsburgh, Pa.
    Saxon, Adams & Co., Pittsburgh, Pa.
    Swan, Bryce Bros., Pittsburgh, Pa.
    Dog, Bryce Bros., Pittsburgh, Pa.
    Bird, Bryce Bros., Pittsburgh, Pa.

Middle Row

    Deer and Dog, Bryce Bros., Pittsburgh, Pa.
    Panelled Daisy, Bryce Bros., Pittsburgh, Pa.
    Rosette, Bryce Bros., Pittsburgh, Pa.
    Fishscale, Bryce Bros., Pittsburgh, Pa.

Bottom Row

    Ribbed Forget-Me-Not, 3¼ oz., Bryce Bros., Pittsburgh, Pa.
    Panelled Hobnail, Bryce Bros., Pittsburgh, Pa.
    Diamond Waffle, 1¾ oz., Bryce Bros., Pittsburgh, Pa.
    Basket Weave, Bryce Bros., Pittsburgh, Pa.
    Looped Panel, Bryce Bros., Pittsburgh, Pa.

PLATE II

Top Row, left to right

    Hanover Star, Medium, 5¼ oz., Richards & Hartley, Tarentum, Pa.
    Hanover Star, Large, 7¾ oz., Richards & Hartley, Tarentum, Pa.
    Three-Panel, Medium, 5¼ oz., Richards & Hartley, Tarentum, Pa.
    Three-Panel, Large, 7¾ oz., Richards & Hartley, Tarentum, Pa.
    Rustic, Gillinder & Sons, Greensburg, Pa.

Middle Row

    Tycoon, Small, 3¾ oz., Columbia Glass Co., Findlay, Ohio
    Tycoon, Medium, 5 oz., Columbia Glass Co., Findlay, Ohio
    Tycoon, Large, 6½ oz., Columbia Glass Co., Findlay, Ohio
    Prism, Cup, Columbia Glass Co., Findlay, Ohio
    Crested Hobnail, Tall, Columbia Glass Co., Findlay, Ohio

Bottom Row

    Stippled Vine, Small, King Glass Co., Pittsburgh, Pa.
    Stippled Vine, Medium, King Glass Co., Pittsburgh, Pa.
    Stippled Vine, Large, King Glass Co., Pittsburgh, Pa.
    Pressed Oak Leaf, Central Glass Co., Wheeling, W. Va.
    Cabbage Rose, Central Glass Co., Wheeling, W. Va.

Catalogue #5 There are several collectors of toy mugs. Here are toy mug examples, many of which came from the United States Glass Company, *Magazine of Old Glass*, Jan. 1940.

PLATE NO. 1

Top Row, left to right

    Crested Hobnail, etched band, 5 oz., A. J. Beatty & Sons, Tiffin, Ohio
    Crested Hobnail, footed, 4½ oz., A. J. Beatty & Sons, Tiffin, Ohio
    Mitred Block, A. J. Beatty & Sons, Tiffin, Ohio
    Mitred Block, lipped, A. J. Beatty & Sons, Tiffin, Ohio
    Spear, A. J. Beatty & Sons, Tiffin, Ohio
    Prism, A. J. Beatty & Sons, Tiffin, Ohio

Middle Row

    Swirl and Ball, A. J. Beatty & Sons, Tiffin, Ohio
    Cut Block and Daisy, Small, Bellaire Goblet Co., Findlay, Ohio
    Cut Block and Daisy, Medium, Bellaire Goblet Co., Findlay, Ohio
    Cut Block and Daisy, Large, Bellaire Goblet Co., Findlay, Ohio
    Cut Block and Daisy, Full size, Bellaire Goblet Co., Findlay, Ohio

Bottom Row

    Hobnail, Rope Handle, Bellaire Goblet Co., Findlay, Ohio
    Reeded Waffle, Bryce Bros., Pittsburgh, Pa.
    Columbia, Columbia Glass Works, Findlay, Ohio
    Daisy and Button, scalloped band, Gillinder & Sons, Greensburg, Pa.
    Lily-of-the-Valley, Bryce Bros., Pittsburgh, Pa.

PLATE III

Top Row, left to right

    Rabbit, Central Glass Co., Wheeling, W. Va.
    Elephant, Central Glass Co., Wheeling, W. Va.
    Faceted, Small, Doyle & Co., Pittsburgh, Pa.
    Faceted, Medium, Doyle & Co., Pittsburgh, Pa.
    Hobnail, notched handle, 5¾ oz., Doyle & Co., Pittsburgh, Pa.

Middle Row

    Hobnail, Thumbprint base, Doyle & Co., Pittsburgh, Pa.
    Pillar and Cut Diamond, Doyle & Co., Pittsburgh, Pa.
    Red Block, Doyle & Co., Pittsburgh, Pa.
    Shell, Doyle & Co., Pittsburgh, Pa.
    Daisy and Button with V-Ornament, Small, A. J. Beatty & Sons, Tiffin, Ohio

Bottom Row

    Daisy and Button with V-Ornament, Medium, A. J. Beatty & Sons, Tiffin, Ohio
    Daisy and Button with V-Ornament, Large, A. J. Beatty & Sons, Tiffin, Ohio
    Daisy and Button with V-Ornament, full-size, A. J. Beatty & Sons, Tiffin, Ohio
    Hobnail, 7 Rows, A. J. Beatty & Sons, Tiffin, Ohio
    Crested Hobnail, cup, 3 oz., A. J. Beatty & Sons, Tiffin, Ohio

No. 2912 Child's Cup $1.50
French grey finish, gold lined.
(K. & O. Co.)

Enlarged illustration
No. 2749 Child's Cup $2.70
Grey, gold lined, subjects on reverse side
"Cock Robin" and "Goosey Gander."
(Homan Silver Plate Co.)

No. 2730 Child's Cup $2.10
Buster Brown, black inlaid, gold lined.
(Homan Silver Plate Co.)

Catalogue #6 Quadruple silver-plated cups for children were popular from 1908-1930. The ones shown here are from an old catalogue of Nordman Brothers Company, Wholesale Jewelers in San Francisco, California.

203

Index

205

Bibliography

Arman, D. and L., *Historical Staffordshire: An Illustrated Check-List,* Danville, Virginia 1974.

Butler Brothers Catalogue Reprints 1905-1930. Chattanooga, Tennessee.

Coleman, Evelyn J. 1914 Marshall Field & Co., *Kringle Society Dolls,* Hobby House Press. Maryland. 1980.

Coysh, A.W. and Henrywood, R.K., *The Dictionary of Blue and White Printed Pottery 1780-1880,* Antique Collectors' Club. England 1982.

Cushion, J.P., *Handbook of Pottery and Porcelain Marks,* Farber & Farber. London and Boston 1956-1980.

Denys Ingram Publishers, *Toys-Dolls-Games Paris 1903-1914.* London. Hastings House Publishers Inc., N.Y. 1981.

Doll and Toy Collector (Magazine Series). Punch Distribution Services. London 1983-1984.

Gates, William C. and Ormerod, Dana E., The East Liverpool, Ohio, Pottery District, The Society for Historical Archaeology. Ohio 1982.

Godden, G.A., *British Pottery: An Illustrated Guide.* London 1974.

Godden, G.A., *Godden's Guide to Mason's China and the Ironstone Wares.* Woodbridge 1980.

Godden, G.A., *An Illustrated Encyclopedia of British Pottery and Porcelain, London 1956.*

Hughes, G.B., English and Scottish Earthenware 1660-1860, London.

Kovel, Know Your Collectibles, Crown Publishers, Inc. N.Y. 1981.

Laidacker, S., *Anglo-American China, Part II,* Bristol, Pa. 1951.

Lechler and O'Neill, *Children's Glass dishes,* Thomas Nelson, Nashville, Tn. 1976.

Lechler, Doris, *Children's Glass Dishes, China and Furniture,* Collector Books, Ky. 1983.

Lee, Ruth Webb, *Sandwich Glass,* Lee Publications, 1939, 1947, 1966, America.

Mandel, Margaret, *Teddy Bears and Steiff Animals,* Collector Books, Ky. 1984.

McClinton, Katharine Morrison, *Antiques in Miniatures.* Scribner's, N.Y. 1970.

McKearin, Geo., and Helen, *American Glass,* Crown, N.Y. 1941, 1948.

Milbourn, Maurice and Evelyn, *Understanding Miniature British Pottery and Porcelain 1730-Present. London 1983.*

Montgomery Ward & Co. (catalogue No. 69), 1901, Research Publications, Tn.

Politzer, Judy and Frank, Tuesday's Children, Politzer, Ca. 1977.

Rontgen, Robert E., *Marks of German, Bohemian and Austrian Porcelain 1710 to the Present..* Pa. Schiffer Publisher 1981.

Schlegelmilch, Clifford J., *RS Prussia.* Michigan, Clifford J. Schlegemilch 1973.

Spillman, Jane, *The Knopf Collectors' Guide to American Antiques: Glass, Vol. 2,* Knopf, N.Y. 1983.

Williams, Petra, *Staffordshire Romantic Transfer Patterns,* Jeffersontown, Ky. 1978.

Williams, Petra, *Flow Blue, I and II,* Jeffersontown, KY 1971, 1973.

Williams, Petra, *Flow Blue China and Mulberry Ware,* Jefferson, KY 1975.

Schroeder's ANTIQUES Price Guide

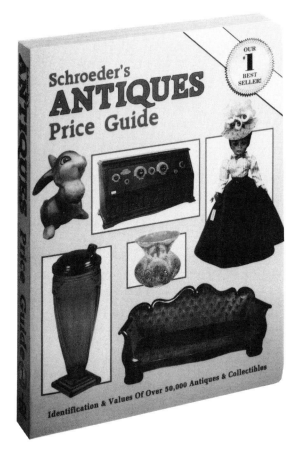

Schroeder's Antiques Price Guide is the #1 best-selling antiques & collectibles value guide on the market today, and here's why . . . More than 300 authors, well-known dealers, and top-notch collectors work together with our editors to bring you accurate information regarding pricing and identification. More than 45,000 items in almost 500 categories are listed along with hundreds of sharp original photos that illustrate not only the rare and unusual, but the common, popular collectibles as well. Each large close-up shot shows important details clearly. Every subject is represented with histories and background information, a feature not found in any of our competitors' publications. Our editors keep abreast of newly-developing trends, often adding several new categories a year as the need arises. If it merits the interest of today's collector, you'll find it in Schroeder's. And you can feel confident that the information we publish is up to date and accurate. Our advisors thoroughly check each category to spot inconsistencies, listings that may not be entirely reflective of market dealings, and lines too vague to be of merit. Only the best of the lot remains for publication. Without doubt, you'll find Schroeder's Antiques Price Guide the only one to buy for reliable information and values.

8½ x 11", 608 Pages

$12.95

COLLECTOR BOOKS
A Division of Schroeder Publishing Co., Inc.